Dr. Eki Aghahowa leads a great church moving forward in kingdom work in a country hostile to Christians, so she is uniquely qualified to speak on the topic, "The Whole Armor of God." As a pastor and a prayer warrior, she understands that what we are fighting with is not flesh and blood, but mindsets, ways, and cultures resistant and even defiant to God and His people. As she teaches, this book will "open up your eyes" (2 Kings 6:17) to the unseen realm believers battle with and must be wise about so they can overcome each and every day!

—Marc Lawson
The 166Life, Founder of Antioch Church
Woodstock, GA USA
www.166factor.com

It is truly a great honor and with great excitement that I get the opportunity to introduce my friend and pastor, *Dr. Eki Aghahowa*, the amazing teacher and apostle in Christ.

Dr. Eki Aghahowa has an intense passion for life, for the people around the world, and for the Word of God. She is one of the most inspiring persons I have come across in my life. Dr. Eki is a laid-down lover of Christ and ultimately makes you aspire to be a better person in your pursuit for Jesus.

Dr. Eki has one mission clearly stated in this book: to tell the world to flow with the full armor of God. We cannot make decisions based on our intellect or on our circumstances. Make decisions from your promise, because Scripture says that from out of our belly, rivers of life flow.

One of my fondest moments of this book is when Dr. Eki reveals the importance of the *whole armor of God* for every believer. She says, "There is no better uniform to put on and wear on a daily basis than the whole armor of God. There is no part of the armor that is supposed to be left out and not worn on a daily basis. It is not just any armor, but God's armor that He has given to the believer. Nothing can come against God's armor and prevail because God never fails. However, we have to have a full knowledge of every component of the whole armor of God because it is only with knowledge that we can put it on and keep it on. You do not go out into the world without it; otherwise, you are naked in the spirit and an easy prey." It is true that when you go out there, you should be ready to stand at any time. Simply ask God to walk with you while you are fitted in the *whole armor of God.*

In this book you will be so much consumed with God that there will be nothing else that matters to you. This is a true reflection of Dr. Eki's life. She is so consumed with Jesus. *The Whole Armor of God* is an amazing book that will take you on a journey. This book will encourage you and leave you with the hunger to pursue more of God. Once you start reading you won't put this book down.

It's real. That place with Him that eclipses everything you can imagine. You can't pursue it by effort…You can only pursue it by following Him! Come put on the *whole armor of God.*

Enjoy the journey…

—Surprise Sithole
International Director of Pastors for IRIS Global
www.surprisesithole.com
www.irisglobal.org
www.irisrevivalchurch.com

WHOLE ARMOR
of GOD

WHOLE ARMOR *of* GOD

EKI AGHAHOWA

CREATION
HOUSE

THE WHOLE ARMOR OF GOD by Eki Aghahowa
Published by Creation House
A Charisma Media Company
600 Rinehart Road
Lake Mary, Florida 32746
www.charismamedia.com

Scripture quotations marked HCSB are taken from the Holman Christian Standard Bible®, Copyright © 1999, 2000, 2002, 2003, 2009 by Holman Bible Publishers. Used by permission. Holman Christian Standard Bible®, Holman CSB®, and HCSB® are federally registered trademarks of Holman Bible Publishers.

Scripture quotations marked CEV are from the Contemporary English Version, copyright © 1995 by the American Bible Society. Used by permission.

Design Director: Justin Evans
Cover design by Judith McKittrick-Wright

Visit the author's website: www.solwmkuwait.org

Library of Congress Cataloging-in-Publication Data:
2015957516
International Standard Book Number: 978-1-62998-509-1
E-book International Standard Book Number:
978-1-62998-510-7

While the author has made every effort to provide accurate telephone numbers and Internet addresses at the time of publication, neither the publisher nor the author assumes any responsibility for errors or for changes that occur after publication.

First edition

16 17 18 19 20 — 9 8 7 6 5 4 3 2 1
Printed in Canada

TABLE *of* CONTENTS

PREFACE

IN THE WORLDLY system, there are certain professions that require people to wear uniforms. By the uniform, you know which profession the individual belongs to. When you see a nurse in the hospital, she does not have to tell you she is a nurse. You know by the uniform she is wearing. It does not matter where in the world you are; you will recognize a nurse in her uniform. She is supposed to perform her nursing duties in the hospital in her uniform. The head nurse in a hospital ward will not allow any nurse perform her function in the ward in worldly clothing, no matter how proficient she is at what she does.

The Lord has given us a heavenly uniform too, which is not made with earthly material. This uniform is not available to those who do not have eyes to see things in the Spirit, or those who do not have an understanding of the Word of God. Even if you have been a believer for thirty years or so and do not have an understanding of the Word of God, you cannot avail yourself of this uniform because you will not know how to lay hold of it. It is the Holy Spirit who gives us understanding of the Word of God, thereby causing the blinders in our spirits to come off. Only then is the Word of God given free rein to do a work in us.

> Brethren, be not children in understanding: how-
> beit in malice be ye children, but in understanding
> be men.
>
> —1 CORINTHIANS 14:20

For every believer, there is no better uniform to put on and wear on a daily basis than the whole armor of God. There is no part of the armor that is supposed to be left unworn on a daily basis. It is not just any armor, but God's armor that He has given to the believer. Nothing can come against God's armor and prevail because God never fails. However, we have to have a full knowledge of every component of the whole armor of God because it is only with knowledge that we can put it on and keep it on. You do not go out into the world without it; otherwise, you are naked in the spirit and an easy prey for the devil.

When you go out without putting the whole armor of God on, you usually come back beaten, bruised, battered, confused, and exhausted. Then you find yourself asking God to heal you—body, soul, and spirit. We need to be wise by using and engaging what God has given to us for our protection. God has ordained every believer to be a warrior in the army of the Lord. God not only calls us, but He also equips, directs, and gives the marching orders.

Are you ready to pursue an understanding of the whole armor of God? Ephesians 6:10–17 is the basis for this book. Let us read it together.

> Finally, my brethren, be strong in the Lord, and in
> the power of his might. Put on the whole armor of
> God, that ye may be able to stand against the wiles
> of the devil. For we wrestle not against flesh and
> blood, but against principalities, against powers,

against the rulers of the darkness of this world, against spiritual wickedness in high places. Wherefore take unto you the whole armor of God, that ye may be able to withstand in the evil day, and having done all, to stand. Stand therefore, having your loins girt about with truth, and having on the breastplate of righteousness; and your feet shod with the preparation of the gospel of peace; above all, taking the shield of faith, wherewith ye shall be able to quench all the fiery darts of the wicked. And take the helmet of salvation, and the sword of the Spirit, which is the word of God.

I pray that the Holy Spirit will enlighten the eyes of your understanding as you go through the pages of this book. God bless you.

—*Dr. Eki Aghahowa*

Chapter 1

WHY *the* WHOLE ARMOR *of* GOD?

But God led the people about, through
the way of the wilderness of the Red
sea: and the children of Israel went up
harnessed out of the land of Egypt.
—Exodus 13:18

THE ISRAELITES WENT out from bondage in Egypt, harnessed. The word *harnessed* means "in battle array" or "armored." Therefore, it means that the Israelites left Egypt spiritually protected. That is how a child of God should be. He should be harnessed in the power of God. The Egyptians did not want to release the Israelites. They were using them to build their nation, but they treated them as slaves. As long as the Israelites were in Egypt, they were not free to worship their God. They did not have any possessions or entitlements in Egypt, but God brought them out with a strong arm. There are certain things that ensnare or entrap us. It may even be the generations before us that mortgaged our freedom, and it

1

needs the strong arm of God to bring us totally out. What the Lord desires for His children is total deliverance in every area of their lives. This is so that nothing has a hold on us except the Lord Himself because a person is subject and slave to anything that controls him. The only one you should be slave to is your Father in heaven. God desires that you come out whole from every ugly situation. You are of no use to yourself and others when you come out fragmented in your soul and spirit. Externally, you might appear whole in your body, but your mind is in tatters. It is only with a sound mind that you can grasp and understand the fullness of God. When you understand the fullness of God, then you understand who you are.

When you are harnessed by God, there is a firm grip on your life and you come out of life's battles intact. When you are harnessed, you can stand. When you are harnessed, nothing can come against you and succeed. It does not matter with what force the enemy pursues you; he cannot reach you, touch you, or knock you down because you are held together by the power of God Almighty. The Israelites lived slightly over four hundred years in slavery in Egypt, but in just one night, God turned them into His army. The Israelites went out of Egypt on foot, while the pursuing Egyptian army came after them in their special chariots. Yet, the Egyptians perished because the Israelites came out harnessed by the hand of God. The power of heaven cannot be compared with that of any other realm. It demolishes all principalities and powers and is higher and greater than any other power. The Israelites went out of Egypt with a high hand, proudly and defiantly, not stealing away like slaves—because they were harnessed by the hand of God. This is further reiterated in the following scriptures.

And the LORD hardened the heart of Pharaoh king of Egypt, and he pursued after the children of Israel: and the children of Israel went out with an high hand.

—EXODUS 14:8

The God of this people of Israel chose our fathers, and exalted the people when they dwelt as strangers in the land of Egypt, and with an high arm brought he them out of it.

—ACTS 13:17

God instructs us in His ways because He has designed us for victory and triumph. The Apostle Paul calls believers "more than conquerors" through Christ Jesus (Rom. 8:37). This denotes the completeness of the victory—not external and temporary, but internal and permanent. Being more than a conqueror means you not only vanquish your foes, but you turn them around to work for your good and to help you accomplish your goals. I am reminded of the continent I come from—Africa. African countries were colonized by the Western world, mainly the British, French, and Portuguese. Where the British colonized, the people retained their native languages and dialects. However, the French were smarter. Wherever the French colonized, they eradicated the native language and made the people speak French until a time came when they could no longer remember their original language. Till this day, French is their first language. They speak French and think French; their food habits are French; and they are still answerable to France. That is what I call a lasting victory!

The just LORD is in the midst thereof; he will not do iniquity: every morning doth he bring his judgment

3

to light, he faileth not; but the unjust knoweth no
shame.

—ZEPHANIAH 3:5

And the LORD, he it is that doth go before thee; he
will be with thee, he will not fail thee, neither forsake thee: fear not, neither be dismayed.

—DEUTERONOMY 31:8

Jesus has a track record of success with no failures.
There are no failures in the kingdom. God does not fail,
and so the kingdom of God does not fail. The kingdom
of God stands forever and is forever expanding; because
it stands, you also stand. Jesus Christ represents the
kingdom of God, and He remains forevermore. We need
to know what God has already planned and assigned to us
for our welfare here on Earth.

And when I saw him, I fell at his feet as dead. And he
laid his right hand upon me, saying unto me, Fear
not; I am the first and the last: I am he that liveth,
and was dead; and, behold, I am alive for evermore,
Amen; and have the keys of hell and of death.

—REVELATION 1:17–18

Then king Darius wrote unto all people, nations,
and languages, that dwell in all the earth; Peace be
multiplied unto you. I make a decree, that in every
dominion of my kingdom men tremble and fear
before the God of Daniel: for he is the living God,
and stedfast for ever, and his kingdom that which
shall not be destroyed, and his dominion shall be
even unto the end.

—DANIEL 6:25–26

A king rules over a kingdom which is his domain. The kingdom of God is in the believer, which means that the domain of God is in you if you are a believer! Therefore, you live, move, and have your being in the domain of God. Wherever you go, you carry the kingdom of God along with you; you are within the domain of God where He is King and rules. The Bible tells us that we are in this world but not of this world (John 15:19; 17:14, 16). We live in the domain of the King of kings and Lord of lords. Jesus knew this, so even though the Jews took up stones to cast at Him, they could not kill Him; instead, Jesus passed through their midst unhurt (John 8:59). They could not lay hands on Him till He willingly gave up His life for humankind. In God's domain, there is no sickness, disease, lack, fear, demons, etc. That is why Jesus told His disciples to preach the gospel of the kingdom of God and heal the sick. He said, "When you heal, tell the one healed that the kingdom of God is here" (see Luke 10:9).

With the whole armor of God, we have victory over principalities, powers, the rulers of the darkness of this world, and spiritual wickedness in high places in Jesus' name. The problem is not the overbearing boss or the difficult job situation, but our not obeying God's Word to put on His whole armor. Do we go out naked without putting any clothing on? Of course not! So why do we think we have any business not putting on the whole armor of God? Put on the whole armor of God, believe that you are wearing every component at all times, and thank God for entrusting you with His armor. We have to be battle ready as David was in 1 Samuel 17:48–49. It must grieve God to see us reject what He has given us for our own protection. By not putting it on, we are telling God, "I do not need

Your armor. I can take care of myself." We end up coming back to God bleeding all over because walking right with God every day is warfare. We cannot do this on our own.

Ephesians 6:10 starts with the word *finally*:

> Finally, my brethren, be strong in the Lord, and in the power of his might.

Paul was invariably saying to the Ephesians, "At the end of my discussion with you; this is my last word to you." The last word said by someone when he is departing is usually the most important word, one that he wants you to remember. It is the word we really need to give an ear to hear and to understand. Paul uses the words "my brethren," so this word is for believers. "Be strong" in Greek is *endunamoó* which means "empowered."[1] The word *power* in Greek is *kratos*, which means "dominion."[2] So, Paul in Ephesians 6:10 was actually saying, "Finally, fellow believers, be empowered in the Lord and be empowered in the dominion of His might." We are to be empowered in the Lord, not in ourselves; and in His might, not ours, because it is His might that has dominion.

I sometimes hear believers say, "I am weak." Of course you are weak. You cannot be strong in yourself except in the Lord. He is your source of strength, so draw strength from Him. Do not be wimpy.

> Hast thou not known? hast thou not heard, that the everlasting God, the LORD, the Creator of the ends of the earth, fainteth not, neither is weary? there is no searching of his understanding. He giveth power to the faint; and to them that have no might he increaseth strength. Even the youths shall faint

and be weary, and the young men shall utterly fall:
but they that wait upon the LORD shall renew their
strength; they shall mount up with wings as eagles;
they shall run, and not be weary; and they shall
walk, and not faint.

—ISAIAH 40:28–31

Therefore shall ye keep all the commandments
which I command you this day, that ye may be
strong, and go in and possess the land, whither
ye go to possess it; and that ye may prolong your
days in the land, which the LORD sware unto your
fathers to give unto them and to their seed, a land
that floweth with milk and honey.

—DEUTERONOMY 11:8–9

Keeping God's commandments makes you strong to
possess what God has given you and prolongs your days
so that you can enjoy what He has given you in the place
He takes you to.

And his name through faith in his name hath made
this man strong, whom ye see and know: yea, the
faith which is by him hath given him this perfect
soundness in the presence of you all.

—ACTS 3:16

Faith in the name of Jesus Christ makes you strong and
gives you perfect soundness.

If ye then be risen with Christ, seek those things
which are above, where Christ sitteth on the right
hand of God. Set your affection on things above, not
on things on the earth. For ye are dead, and your life

is hid with Christ in God. When Christ, who is our life, shall appear, then shall ye also appear with him in glory. Mortify therefore your members which are upon the earth; fornication, uncleanness, inordinate affection, evil concupiscence, and covetousness, which is idolatry: For which things' sake the wrath of God cometh on the children of disobedience: in the which ye also walked some time, when ye lived in them. But now ye also put off all these; anger, wrath, malice, blasphemy, filthy communication out of your mouth. Lie not one to another, seeing that ye have put off the old man with his deeds; and have put on the new man, which is renewed in knowledge after the image of him that created him:

—COLOSSIANS 3:1–10

For if ye live after the flesh, ye shall die: but if ye through the Spirit do mortify the deeds of the body, ye shall live.

—ROMANS 8:13

The devil will have no foothold in our lives if our flesh does not cooperate with him. We need to mortify our flesh daily by the Holy Spirit so that we will not heed to demonic manipulation. Dead men are incapable of responding. This is the power of a crucified life. Living a crucified life is a crucial part of spiritual warfare; otherwise, your flesh will be your greatest enemy.

For the love of Christ constraineth us; because we thus judge, that if one died for all, then were all dead: and that he died for all, that they which live

should not henceforth live unto themselves, but
unto him which died for them, and rose again.
—2 Corinthians 5:14–15

It is not enough for us to be dead; we also need to be buried with Him. The old nature has to go under the earth where it belongs, never to be experienced again. Some of us still have problems with areas of our lives which we have professed to be dead because the old nature is not buried. If it was, it would be completely out of sight. When you profess to be dead, but you are not buried with Christ, then you are a dead man walking and stumbling all the time instead of being a quickened spirit in Christ, living unto God. The first man Adam, after sinning in the Garden of Eden, walked about with a spirit that was dead unto God (Gen. 2:17). However, Jesus came as a quickening spirit (1 Cor. 15:45), and it is in the image of Him that the new creation is created. Without death and burial, there can be no quickening.

Thou fool, that which thou sowest is not quickened,
except it die:
—1 Corinthians 15:36

No one goes to the graveyard for a picnic, and nobody voluntarily goes to the grave. Death leads one to the grave. It is the things we go through that take us to the grave where issues in our lives are exposed and the members of our old man are mortified by the Holy Spirit. Jesus learnt obedience by the things He suffered and was made perfect to become the author of eternal salvation unto all who obey Him (Heb. 5:8). In the grave experience, God speaks to us in the dark places of our lives, and we are to tell of these things in the light (Matt. 10:27). In the grave, the Holy Spirit helps us confront issues with the Word of God. These issues include the following:

ANGER

Confronting Word:

> An angry man stirreth up strife, and a furious man aboundeth in transgression.
> —PROVERBS 29:22

> But I say to you that everyone who continues be to angry with his brother or harbors malice (enmity of heart) against him shall be liable to and unable to escape the punishment imposed by the court; and whoever speaks contemptuously and insultingly to his brother shall be liable to and unable to escape the punishment imposed by the Sanhedrin, and whoever says, You cursed fool! [You empty-headed idiot!] shall be liable to and unable to escape the hell (Gehenna) of fire.
> —MATTHEW 5:22, AMP

Solution:

> Be ye angry, and sin not: let not the sun go down upon your wrath: neither give place to the devil.
> —EPHESIANS 4:26–27

> He that is slow to anger is better than the mighty; and he that ruleth his spirit than he that taketh a city.
> —PROVERBS 16:32

BITTERNESS

Confronting Word:

> Looking diligently lest any man fail of the grace of God; lest any root of bitterness springing up trouble you, and thereby many be defiled;
>
> —HEBREWS 12:15

Solution:

> Let all bitterness, and wrath, and anger, and clamour, and evil speaking, be put away from you, with all malice: and be ye kind one to another, tenderhearted, forgiving one another, even as God for Christ's sake hath forgiven you.
>
> —EPHESIANS 4:31–32

COVETOUSNESS

Confronting Word:

> But fornication, and all uncleanness, or covetousness, let it not be once named among you, as becometh saints...For this ye know, that no whoremonger, nor unclean person, nor covetous man, who is an idolater, hath any inheritance in the kingdom of Christ and of God.
>
> —EPHESIANS 5:3, 5

Solution:

> Let your character or moral disposition be free from love of money [including greed, avarice, lust,

and craving for earthly possessions] and be satisfied with your present [circumstances and with what you have]; for He [God] Himself has said, I will not in any way fail you nor give you up nor leave you without support. [I will] not, [I will] not, [I will] not in any degree leave you helpless nor forsake nor let [you] down (relax My hold on you)! [Assuredly not!]

—HEBREWS 13:5, AMP

But godliness with contentment is great gain. For we brought nothing into this world, and it is certain we can carry nothing out. And having food and raiment let us be therewith content. But they that will be rich fall into temptation and a snare, and into many foolish and hurtful lusts, which drown men in destruction and perdition. For the love of money is the root of all evil: which while some coveted after, they have erred from the faith, and pierced themselves through with many sorrows.

—1 TIMOTHY 6:6–10

SLANDER

Confronting Word:

Whoever slanders their neighbour in secret, I will put to silence; whoever has haughty eyes and a proud heart, I will not tolerate.

—PSALM 101:5, NIV

Brothers and sisters, do not slander one another. Anyone who speaks against a brother or sister or judges them speaks against the law and judges it. When you judge the law, you are not keeping it, but sitting in judgment on it. There is only one Lawgiver and Judge, the one who is able to save and destroy. But you—who are you to judge your neighbor?

—James 4:11–12, niv

Solution:

Watch your tongue and keep your mouth shut, and you will stay out of trouble.

—Proverbs 21:23, nlt

A wholesome tongue is a tree of life: but perverseness therein is a breach in the spirit.

—Proverbs 15:4

LYING

Confronting Word:

But the fearful, and unbelieving, and the abominable, and murderers, and whoremongers, and sorcerers, and idolaters, and all liars, shall have their part in the lake which burneth with fire and brimstone: which is the second death.

—Revelation 21:8

Solution:

These are the things that ye shall do; speak ye every man the truth to his neighbour; execute the judgment of truth and peace in your gates: And let none of you imagine evil in your hearts against his neighbour; and love no false oath: for all these are things that I hate, saith the LORD.

—ZECHARIAH 8:16–17

LUST

Confronting Word:

Love not the world, neither the things that are in the world. If any man love the world, the love of the Father is not in him. For all that is in the world, the lust of the flesh, and the lust of the eyes, and the pride of life, is not of the Father, but is of the world. And the world passeth away, and the lust thereof: but he that doeth the will of God abideth for ever.

—1 JOHN 2:15–17

When you follow the desires of your sinful nature, the results are very clear: sexual immorality, impurity, lustful pleasures, idolatry, sorcery, hostility, quarreling, jealousy, outbursts of anger, selfish ambition, dissension, division, envy, drunkenness, wild parties, and other sins like these. Let me tell you again, as I have before, that anyone living that sort of life will not inherit the Kingdom of God.

—GALATIANS 5:19–21, NLT

Solution:

This I say then, Walk in the Spirit, and ye shall not fulfil the lust of the flesh. For the flesh lusteth against the Spirit, and the Spirit against the flesh: and these are contrary the one to the other: so that ye cannot do the things that ye would. But if ye be led of the Spirit, ye are not under the law....But the fruit of the Spirit is love, joy, peace, longsuffering, gentleness, goodness, faith, meekness, temperance: against such there is no law. And they that are Christ's have crucified the flesh with the affections and lusts. If we live in the Spirit, let us also walk in the Spirit.

—GALATIANS 5:16–18, 22–25

Finally, brothers and sisters, whatever is true, whatever is noble, whatever is right, whatever is pure, whatever is lovely, whatever is admirable—if anything is excellent or praiseworthy—think about such things.

—PHILIPPIANS 4:8, NIV

PRIDE

Confronting Word:

Every one that is proud in heart is an abomination to the LORD: though hand join in hand, he shall not be unpunished.

—PROVERBS 16:5

Solution:

Humble yourselves therefore under the mighty hand of God, that he may exalt you in due time: casting all your care upon him; for he careth for you.

—1 PETER 5:6–7

Let this mind be in you, which was also in Christ Jesus: who, being in the form of God, thought it not robbery to be equal with God: but made himself

of no reputation, and took upon him the form of
a servant, and was made in the likeness of men:
and being found in fashion as a man, he humbled
himself, and became obedient unto death, even the
death of the cross.

—PHILIPPIANS 2:5–8

It is in the grave that we are delivered of things that
hold us captive, for as our members die to sin and are
buried, there is nothing for the devil to hold on to in our
lives, just as he had nothing in Jesus to hold on to (John
14:30). We come out of the grave not like Lazarus with his
grave clothes that needed to be loosed by others around
him, but as Jesus came out of the grave leaving behind His
grave clothes. To be completely loosened from the grave
clothes (which means being completely delivered from all
captivity by the power of God that we experience in His
Word while in the grave) we have to endure the grave till
the fullness of time ordained by God, just as Jesus spent
three days and nights in the grave.

You are a living sacrifice unto God, and that is your rea-
sonable service to Him (Rom. 12:1). Have you ever seen a
sacrifice struggling to get off the altar? Any animal sacri-
ficed is dead. However, you are living because God's Spirit
is in you. It is His Spirit in us that causes us to live. We must
allow the Holy Spirit do a complete work in our lives so that
we come out of the grave with areas of our captivity con-
quered by using the Word of God. While in the grave, the
Lord builds us up on the foundation of who He is as the Son
of God and the Word of God. Just as Jesus came out of the
grave with the keys of death and hell, we too arise out of the
grave with the keys of the kingdom of God, and these keys
are the Word of God to unlock our breakthrough.

Whatever was holding us captive loses its sting in our lives. It is no longer able to hurt, harm, or overcome us. Keys denote ownership and control. A key is an emblem of authority and evidence of possession. God has given us the keys of the kingdom in His Word and therefore all heavens' resources are made available to us. His divine power gives us all things that pertain to life and godliness through the knowledge of Christ who has called us to glory and excellence (2 Pet. 1:3). We come out of the grave having the mind of Christ—not Jesus the Son of man, but Jesus the Son of God, the Messiah of the world, our Savior, Lord, Master, and Redeemer. We have the mind of the Son of God because we are now sons of God!

Jesus died as the Son of man, but rose as the Son of God. Therefore, when we die with Him and rise with Him, we are as He is, sons of God with His mind. We are able to do what He did and greater because His Spirit is in us and He has ascended to His Father's right hand where He is eternally interceding for us (John 14:12). Old things have passed away, are dead and buried, and all things are now new and of God (2 Cor. 5:17–18). Now, we can walk in heavenly places in Christ Jesus. This is a walk of complete obedience to God with no more struggles because our members are dead and buried, our lives are hid in Christ, and we have the keys of the kingdom. The devil still tempts us, but we have the keys to overcome him. Now, we can partake of the heavenly calling to which we have been called (Heb. 3:1). Now we can ascend to our heavenly places of seating in Christ (Eph. 2:6) where God has blessed us with all spiritual blessings (Eph. 1:3)—and while we are still living physically on Earth, we can identify with what Jesus said in John 3:13.

And no man hath ascended up to heaven, but he
that came down from heaven, even the Son of man
which is in heaven.

Jesus was on Earth, yet He referred to Himself as being
in heaven.

Know ye not, that so many of us as were baptized
into Jesus Christ were baptized into his death?
Therefore we are buried with him by baptism into
death: that like as Christ was raised up from the
dead by the glory of the Father, even so we also
should walk in newness of life. For if we have been
planted together in the likeness of his death, we shall
be also in the likeness of his resurrection: knowing
this, that our old man is crucified with him, that
the body of sin might be destroyed, that henceforth we should not serve sin. For he that is dead
is freed from sin. Now if we be dead with Christ,
we believe that we shall also live with him: knowing
that Christ being raised from the dead dieth no
more; death hath no more dominion over him. For
in that he died, he died unto sin once: but in that
he liveth, he liveth unto God. Likewise reckon ye
also yourselves to be dead indeed unto sin, but alive
unto God through Jesus Christ our Lord. Let not sin
therefore reign in your mortal body, that ye should
obey it in the lusts thereof. Neither yield ye your
members as instruments of unrighteousness unto
sin: but yield yourselves unto God, as those that are
alive from the dead, and your members as instruments of righteousness unto God. For sin shall not

have dominion over you: for ye are not under the
law, but under grace.

—Romans 6:3–14

Our flesh and souls need to be submitted to the Holy
Spirit.

Submit yourselves therefore to God. Resist the devil,
and he will flee from you.

—James 4:7

One day, as we were praying corporately in the church at
a prayer meeting and asking the Lord to occupy our hearts,
thoughts, and intentions—to occupy our temple—the Lord
showed me a vision of a house with many rooms. The word
occupy means that a person totally fills a place; there is
no space for any other thing. This is what our hearts' cry
should be—that the Lord will occupy us. When a house
is occupied, the notice saying there is vacancy is removed;
when people pass by, they have no inclination to come in
because the house is occupied. But I was seeing that some
people were not fully occupied; not all of their rooms were
occupied, and notices bearing the words "Vacancies are
here" were still in front of their buildings. So, when lust
walks by, he says, "There is room for me to enter," and he
enters. When jealousy walks by, he says, "Oh, there is room,"
and he enters. As long as the house is not fully occupied,
whatever is passing by has a legal right to enter because the
vacancy notice has not been removed. It is only when the
house is fully occupied that the vacancy notice is removed.
First, the Lord has to occupy for the vacancy notice to be
removed. As long as the house is not fully occupied, the
vacancy notice has legal right to remain. Pray that the Lord
occupies and fills every room in your life. Let every room

be filled with Him so that nothing can creep in. That is why the Bible says in 1 Corinthians 3:16 that we are the temple of God. Nothing occupied the temple except the presence of God. He told the Israelites to build Him a holy place of habitation, a place that He would occupy amongst them (Exod. 25:8). It is time for our temples to be invaded with the presence of God.

In the parable that Jesus told His disciples in Luke 6:47–49, something happened when the first man mentioned obeyed the Word of God that he heard. He dug deep and laid the foundation of his house on a mass of rock, which in Greek is *petra*. When he obeyed the Word, there was an implosion of the Word in him. An implosion is an explosion inward. It is a force opposite to, but many more times more powerful than an explosion. In a building implosion, the support structure of the building is removed at a certain point using dynamite, high velocity explosives. The section of the building above that point will fall down on the part of the building below that point, and gravity (which is a law) brings the building down. The building collapses onto its footprint which is the total area at the base of the building, while other structures around it are preserved. Virtually every building in the world is unique, even though some may look alike. Therefore, the implosion technique for a building has to be unique for that building.

The word *dynamite* is derived from the Greek word *dunamis*.[3] The Word of God is saturated with the dunamis of God, which is the inherent power of God that reproduces itself in us. Doing God's Word ignites the inherent power of God in it, just as if you ignited dynamite, causing an implosion of the Word in your building, which is your body. This is a controlled inward explosion in you pertaining to the confines of that particular Word, causing the Word to go beyond your flesh (which is the sand in the parable in Luke 6:47–49) to your spirit which is created in the image and likeness of God, the eternal Rock of ages. Therefore, the foundation of what is built as a result of obeying the Word of God is of the spirit and not the flesh, so it stands and does not fall to ruin when the rains, flood, and tempest beat vehemently on it! In the spirit, it is the law of faith (Rom. 3:27) that is operational; this law pulls down anything that attempts to raise itself higher than the Word of God. Jesus is in the business of building in the spirit and not in the flesh, and what He builds in the spirit, the powers of hell cannot prevail against. What is built in flesh immediately falls to ruin when trouble comes.

Philippians 2:12 tells us to work out our salvation by obeying God's Word. The Message Bible calls it responsive obedience to the Word of God. Success is not whether you have a large ministry or business; it is doing what God tells you to do. Whenever we hear the Word of God, we are building, but the pertinent question is, "Where are we building—in the spirit or the flesh?" The parable describes the man who built the foundation of his house on the mass of rock as wise and the one who built his house on sand as foolish (Matt. 7:24, 26). The word *foolish* in Greek is *móros*, which means "blockhead."[4] We do not want to be described as blockheads. The Word of God is preached to your spirit and not flesh as the Word is spirit and life. Spirit speaks to spirit, and it is only spirit that understands things of the spirit.

The Word of God, which is seed, will not produce a harvest till you plant it. The ground in which it is planted is your spirit, and this is done through understanding. It is the Word understood through revelation by the Holy Spirit that gets planted. To plant a seed, you have to break the surface of the ground and dig; then, you cover up the seed with soil so it will not be lost, and then you water it. Whatever you let into your spirit will grow.

Hebrews 1:3 tells us that Jesus upholds, makes stand, and sustains all things by the Word of His power. In obeying the Word of God, you are no longer just holding onto the Word of God, but you are allowing the Word of God to hold you. We have to go beyond holding onto the Word of God to letting it hold us! In Luke 6:48, it was the mass of rock that held the house that was built on it from shaking or falling to ruin. Remember the story of Noah? Noah walked with God and was perfect in a perverse generation where all walked in rebellion to God. He was obedient to God in all his ways. Noah received a Word from God and in obedience, built an ark according to all that God commanded—the emphasis is on *all* (Gen. 6:22, 7:5, 9, 16). Noah held onto the Word of God, doing all of it till what he held onto held himself and his family. When we move by God's revealed Word, we can construct an ark of safety for us and our families. James 1:25 tells us that when we obey God's Word, we are blessed in that particular deed.

> And He Himself existed before all things, and in Him all things consist (cohere, are held together).
> —COLOSSIANS 1:17, AMP

The devil is not omnipresent. He is a created being. The real battle was won at the Resurrection by Jesus Christ, and it is He who defeated the devil that lives in us. Our understanding of spiritual warfare must begin with the knowledge that Jesus has already accomplished victory over Satan. Therefore, we are not seeking victory but enforcing the already won victory. The normal Christian life is a life of victory.

> Forasmuch then as the children are partakers of flesh and blood, he also himself likewise took part of the same; that through death he might destroy him that had the power of death, that is, the devil.
>
> —HEBREWS 2:14

> He that committeth sin is of the devil; for the devil sinneth from the beginning. For this purpose the Son of God was manifested, that he might destroy the works of the devil.
>
> —1 JOHN 3:8

There is nothing we can add to the destructive work Jesus has already done to Satan and his domain.

> Put on the whole armor of God, that ye may be able to stand against the wiles of the devil.
>
> —EPHESIANS 6:11

Put on in Greek is *enduō* which means "to sink into clothing." This means God's armor is fixed, but you have to make every adjustment possible in your life to conform to the Word of God to be able to sink into it. The *whole armor* in Greek is *panoplia* which means the "full armor of a heavily armed soldier." The type of outfit a soldier wears depends on the task at hand. The nature of his outfit tells the onlookers the intensity of warfare that soldier is expecting to contend with. A well-trained soldier prefers to be overprepared for an onslaught rather than unprepared in order to ensure victory and come out unhurt. Paul is therefore saying, "Because of the task at hand for every believer, and because of the daily warfare that comes your way (as a result of your full surrender to Christ), you cannot afford to be a scantily dressed soldier. You have to be properly covered and protected. You should not go out in a T-shirt and tennis shoes because the devil will tear you to shreds. As you are a soldier in the army of God, the Lord has given you His armor, which is heavily armed. Therefore, put on the whole armor of God."

This armor is of God, and our God is a God of purpose. You might ask, "Why should I put on God's whole armor?" The answer is, "So that you may be able to stand against the wiles of the devil; the different methods, means, plans, and schemes used by the devil to deceive, entrap, enslave, and ruin man." This is what we encounter in the world on a daily basis. The devil wants to deceive, entrap, enslave, and harm us. He has no good plans for us. He comes to kill, steal, and destroy, but the Lord Jesus has come to give us life and that we may have it more abundantly (John 10:10).

God has not only made the new creation in the likeness of Christ, but He has also given him His whole armor to preserve himself, even in the highest level of warfare. God knows everything. What God does is complete, and you cannot find fault with it. We have one common enemy— the devil. So, we need to stop fighting individuals. We are to resist the methods, different means, plans, and schemes used to deceive, entrap, enslave, and ruin the souls of men.

Ephesians 6:12 gives us a note of caution and some information:

> For we wrestle not against flesh and blood, but against principalities, against powers, against the

rulers of the darkness of this world, against spiritual wickedness in high places.

Paul is saying, "Be it known to you that you are not wrestling, struggling, in conflict, or fighting against man, that which you see or that which is natural, but against the following":

- Principalities (Greek: *archas*) which means chief rulers of the highest rank and order in Satan's kingdom.

- Powers (Greek: *exousias*) which means authorities and those who derive their power from and execute the will of the chief rulers.

- Rulers of the darkness of this world (Greek: *kosmokratopas*) which means world-rulers of the darkness of this age.

- Spiritual wickedness in high places (Greek: *pneumatika ponerias*) which means spiritual wickedness in the heavenlies.[5]

You are not only fighting chief rulers of the highest rank and order in Satan's kingdom, but also those who have been delegated by these chief rulers and have been given their authority to execute their will against you. This hierarchy within the satanic kingdom mentioned in Ephesians 6:12 is comprised of different demonic strata. Some of us wonder why we keep going from warfare to warfare. It is because we are dealing with a multifarious demonic onslaught. There is nothing in this earthly realm that we can use to fight in order to overcome these demonic forces, except we put on the whole armor of God.

> Wherefore take unto you the whole armor of God, that ye may be able to withstand in the evil day, and having done all, to stand.
> —EPHESIANS 6:13

Paraphrased, this verse reads, "Therefore, knowing this, take unto you (this is personal, and it is for every believer) the whole armor of God not leaving any item out. This is so that you may be able to stand against, oppose, and resist the wiles of the devil in the evil, calamitous day and day of moral culpability—the day a loved one dies, the day you get a bad report from the doctor, the day you are involved in a car crash, the day you lose your job, the day you are served with divorce papers even though you still want the marriage—and having done all the withstanding, to stand your place in God. Do not give place to the devil." You are not to wait for the evil day to come before you put on the whole armor of God. You put it on *now*. A soldier does not wait for there to be war before putting on his uniform.

God created you to stand irrespective of the terrain you find yourself in. The word *stand* in Greek is *histémi* which is a prolonged form of the primary word *stao*, and means to stand and keep on standing, to cause a person or thing to keep his or its place, to stand immovable, to stand unharmed, or to be of a steadfast mind.[6]

> Not for that we have dominion over your faith, but are helpers of your joy: for by faith ye stand.
> —2 CORINTHIANS 1:24

You stand and keep on standing by faith. Your faith is the victory that overcomes, subdues, and conquers the world (1 John 5:4). Therefore, when you stand in faith, you stand in victory! If you do not stand firmly in faith, then you will not stand at all.

> The head of Aram is Damascus, the head of Damascus is Rezin (within 65 years Ephraim will be too shattered to be a people), the head of Ephraim is Samaria, and the head of Samaria is the son of Remaliah. If you do not stand firm in your faith, then you will not stand at all.
>
> —ISAIAH 7:8–9, HCSB

As the Israelites were crossing the Jordan River to the Promised Land under the leadership of Joshua, the priests carrying the ark of the covenant stood firm on dry ground in the midst of the river (Josh. 3:17). They did not lose their footing. As a result, all the people passed over the Jordan on dry ground. Standing firm in God requires us to have absolute faith in Him, not doubting His Word. It is your faith that makes the ground level for you to stand on. It is your faith that beats the mountains low, fills the valleys and makes them level, makes the crooked places straight and the rough places smooth and even, and the glory of the Lord shall be revealed (Isa. 40:4–5). Your usefulness to God is dependent on your ability to stand in the face of opposition.

You should dispose of everything you have used as a crutch in your life. Everything you are leaning on, everything you are using as support, you should let go of. God alone is your support, and He is able to make you stand. He is able to make you walk. He is able to make you run. If you allow God to be your only support, you shall run and not be weary because every step of the way, He strengthens you. As you run, you are not running alone because He is running with you. When He told you to run the race (Heb. 12:1), He did not intend you to run it without Him. You cannot run it without Him. You cannot accomplish that which He calls you to without Him. You cannot endure the hardship of the race without Him because He is the very life that runs in your veins. He is your life support. Everything that you may lean on—your finances, family, and possessions shall wear away, but God remains forever. He is the beginning and the ending of all things, the first and the last, the Alpha and Omega. You cannot find God's beginning, and you cannot find His ending. He is infinite. He is eternal. Do you not know that everything in the world is temporal? Therefore, anything or anyone in the world that you are leaning on is temporal. Also, everything that is temporal needs adjustments from time to time, but in God, there are no adjustments because He remains constant forever—He is the same yesterday, today, and forever.

Whatever is in the world is created, and God is the Creator. How can you, a created being, lean on that which is also created? What is created shall fade away (Isa. 24:4, 64:6), but God's Word endures forever (Isa. 40:8). He is the One that created the foundations of the Earth and put the Earth on the pillars upon which they stand. These pillars do not fall because He formed them. Let God be the pillar on which you stand because when you stand upon Him, you shall never fall. He does not shake; there is no variableness in Him or in His Word. He is your constancy, your firm support, and your firm foundation. There is no unsteadiness in God. You cannot be toppled when you cleave to Him. You cannot stumble when you are rooted in Him because He does not stumble.

The Bible says that God has given His angels charge over you, to carry you so that you do not hit your foot against a stone (Ps. 91:11–12). This is because it is only that which is visible that you see with your physical eyes, but there are greater things that are unseen than those that are seen. That is why God has given His angels charge over you to direct you in all your ways. You cannot direct yourself because on your own you do not know the way to go, but the all-knowing and all-seeing God has committed His angels to you to direct you in all your ways. The angels make no error because God gives them the directions. So, He says, "Today will you allow them direct you?" When they direct you, they also clear the way for you because they know that your strength is little. There is no darkness in heaven, but always light. We need to stand and walk in the light of God.

God has given you His whole armor to withstand the wiles of the devil; after you have fought the good fight of faith, you will not be battered or come out panting and gasping with scratches, bruises, and deep cuts. Some of us win the battle, but come out of it wounded, bleeding, and licking our wounds in self pity, bitter and paranoid that everyone is against us and after us. You should be so fit that you will stand and keep on standing ready to take on other onslaughts. God knew that what would be coming against His children were principalities and not a principality; powers and not a power, rulers and not a ruler; and spiritual wickedness in high places, and not just in one high place. Therefore, He has given you His whole armor so that having done all the withstanding, you will remain standing. This is how you know a warrior or a sea-soned soldier. No matter what comes his way, he keeps on standing. You are not to be thrown off balance, deterred, or distracted from your main purpose and goal in God by the ensuing battle.

You never come out of a battle the same as you went in. You come out either better or bitter. Which one do you choose? You have to choose to come out better even before you engage in warfare; otherwise, things you encounter in the course of battle can make you bitter. Therefore, before you go into battle, purpose in your heart how you are going to come out—whole and better than how you went in. Your life is not a reflection of what has happened to you, but a reflection of your responses to them.

The man whom God chose to lead the Israelites into the Promised Land after Moses' death was not the phi-losopher in the camp or the best orator, but the most sea-soned warrior—Joshua. God has given us individual tasks that we can only achieve if we are seasoned warriors. A seasoned warrior does not get weary despite the heat of the battle because he has been trained by exercise to stand, irrespective of how long the battle takes. A warrior is always in a ready state to fight. That is why he keeps fit—so that when the enemy comes, he can fight the enemy down and win. We keep fit by prayer and the written and spoken Word of God.

We are to withstand, resist, and oppose demonic onslaughts—and having done all, to stand! We need to be skilled and seasoned soldiers in the army of God.

ENDNOTES

1. See www.e-sword.net or www.biblehub.com/strongs .htm for quick reference to *Strong's Exhaustive Concordance* for Hebrew and Greek words online; *Endunamoó*, "empowered," Strong's G1743.

2. *Kratos*, "dominion," Strong's G2904.

3. *American Heritage Dictionary*, 5th ed., s.v., "dynamite."

4. *Móros*, "blockhead," Strong's G3474.

5. Finis Dake, *Dake's Annotated Reference Bible* (Atlanta, GA: Dake Bible Sales, 1963), 214.

6. *Histémi*, "to stand," Strong's G2476.

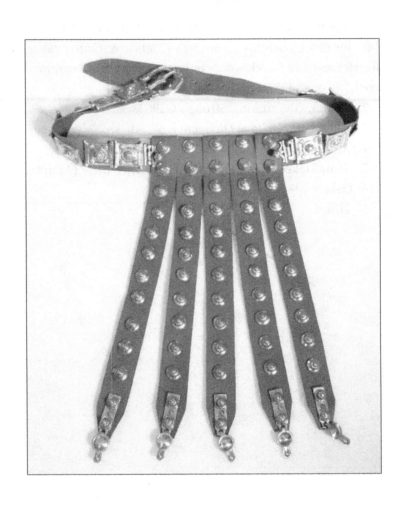

Chapter 2

BELT *of* TRUTH

*Stand therefore, having your loins
girt about with truth, and having on
the breastplate of righteousness.*
—EPHESIANS 6:14

THIS VERSE IS based on what is read prior in Ephesians 6:10–13. According to the *American Heritage Dictionary*, the word *truth* means what is true in any matter under consideration. The word *true* means "in accordance with fact or reality; actual, real, and not false; genuine; in accordance with an original or standard, proper, correct, or exact."[1]

> I have many things to say and to judge of you: but he that sent me is true; and I speak to the world those things which I have heard of him.
>
> —JOHN 8:26

Jesus' witness of God is that He is true. Can you have a better witness of God than Jesus? It does not matter what is going on in your life; God remains true and cannot lie (Num. 23:19; Titus 1:2). We know who is the liar and the father of lies—the devil in whom there is no truth (John 8:44). Jesus is the truth, and He is the only way to the Father who is true (John 14:6). It is only truth that can lead to the One who is true. A lie cannot lead to the One who is true. Truth is never at the mercy of a lie. A lie is a false declaration, distorted fact, or fabricated statement used to deceive or give an incorrect perception. The Greek word for a *lie* is *pseudologos*, which means speaking falsely.[2] Anytime you believe a lie, you empower the liar.

> Then said Jesus to those Jews which believed on him, If ye continue in my word, then are ye my disciples indeed; and ye shall know the truth, and the truth shall make you free.
> —JOHN 8:31–32

This statement is made to those who believe in Jesus. You have to continue believing in His Word daily for the rest of your life. Some of our struggles are related to our not continuing in the Word. When you continue in the Word, you are continuing in Jesus because Jesus is the Word of God. In times of despondency, we tend to say things like, "It is so difficult for me to read the Bible now." Open the Bible and read it. If it means you have to stare at the words, then do so till the Holy Spirit gives you a revelation of the Word. Revelation creates entry into the Word. Meditation on the revealed Word causes an abiding in it and therefore an abiding in Christ. The word *continue* in Greek is *menó* which means to stay in a given place, state, relation, or expectancy.[3] You are to stay, abide, dwell, or remain expectant in the Word of God. Nothing should take you away from the Word of God. That is how you follow Jesus and learn from Him. If you do this, then you will know truth which will make you free. *Knowing* comes out of relationship. Knowing truth is born out of a relationship with Jesus.

The word *know* in John 8:32 in Greek is *ginóskó* which means "to understand."[4] Understanding the truth makes you free. The truth is not found outside the Word of God. It is not found on the pages of the newspaper or on the internet or in much reading. The truth is found only in the person of Jesus Christ and revealed in Him because Jesus is the truth. Hence, His Spirit is the Spirit of truth. You cannot fight the good fight of faith (1 Tim. 6:12) when you are all bound up in sin and believing the lies of the devil. Have you ever seen anyone with bound hands and feet being able to fight? It is only Jesus who can make one free from sin (John 8:31–36). You have to be free to be able to fight; therefore, the first item you put on is the belt of truth.

The phrase "make you free" means to liberate; exempt from moral, ceremonial, or mortal liability; or deliver. Truth makes you free from what? The answer is found in John 8:34, 36. It makes you free from slavery to sin. This promise is for the believer who continues in the Word of God. There is deliverance in the Word of God. The devil does not want you to be free from slavery to sin, so he prevents you from knowing the truth by causing you not to continue in the Word of God. He brings all things your way to distract you from the Word of God. At the end of the day, you are mentally and physically exhausted, and you say, "Tomorrow, I will read my Bible." Tomorrow becomes a week which becomes a month, and then your reading of the Word becomes seasonal. It gets to the point where you do not even know where your Bible is—and you get to look for it on Sunday or whenever you are preparing to go to church. Before I became a believer, I used to put my Bible under my pillow, and I thought that was how I would be protected. Somehow, I thought that the Word would get out of the Bible and permeate me by osmosis. It does not happen like that. You have to read the Word of God. It is not enough for us to profess Jesus if He is not depicted in our lifestyles. How are you living? Are you still a professional sinner? What is truth? The Word of God (John 17:17). Who is truth? The Word of God—Jesus Christ (John 14:6). Grace and truth came through Jesus Christ (John 1:17). When people come to me for counseling with an issue pertaining to sin, the question I usually ask is, "When was the last time you read your Bible?" This is because when you continue in the Word and you are being tempted, the Word of God in you will arise against the lie you are seeing and hearing. However, when there is no Word in you, flesh succumbs to the temptation. It is not the crisis that is the problem, but the lack of continuing in the Word of God.

> Thy word have I hid in mine heart, that I might not sin against thee.
> —PSALM 119:11

When you meditate on the Word of God day and night, you will remember to do all God's Word and therein make your way prosperous and have good success in all your endeavors (Josh. 1:8). Meditation on the Word of God is spiritual digestion of the Word of God which leads to revelation of the truth by the Holy Spirit who is the Spirit of truth. You can only digest and be one with the Word of

God when you meditate on it. "Girt about" in Ephesians 6:14 in Greek is *perizónnumi,* which means to gird all around or to fasten on one's belt.[5] A belt which is buckled is put around the Jewish Torah, which is the belt of truth; the Torah being the Word of God, which is truth.

Girding up one's loins denotes a state of alertness in the spirit, and this can only be done by the Word of God. Hence, the girding of the loins is by the belt of truth. You go to battle fully alert and not half asleep. You should not go to battle without having any discernment of the enemy and his tactics.

In the Holy Place, the table of shewbread was directly opposite the seven candlesticks which represent the fullness of the Holy Spirit: the Spirit of the Lord, the Spirit of wisdom and understanding, the Spirit of counsel and might, and the Spirit of knowledge and of the fear of the Lord (Isa. 11:2). The fullness of the Holy Spirit always shone on the shewbread, and only the priests could eat it once a week on the Sabbath. When they ate the shewbread, they had to eat it in the holy place (Lev. 24:8–9). They could not take it home to eat. The shewbread was replaced every Sabbath (1 Chron. 9:32). Therefore, it meant that for seven days the fullness of the Holy Spirit had illuminated the shewbread the priests ate, and this took them till the next Sabbath. Every believer is a king and priest unto God through Jesus Christ (Rev. 1:6), and our shewbread is the Word of God. The way we eat it is to allow the Holy Spirit to illuminate the Word of God so that the truth in the Word is revealed to us. It is this revealed truth (rhéma) we eat and digest, and it is this that sustains us from day to day. The revealed truth of the Word of God renews the spirit of our minds so that we might have the mind of Christ, the mind of the Messiah, the mind of the King of kings.

I often wondered when reading Ephesians 6:14 why the belt of truth was the first item we are instructed to put on in the whole armor of God. Why not put on the breast-plate first? After all, we wear our shirt or dress before we put on our belt. The following is what the Holy Spirit told me: "The Word of truth sanctifies, makes holy, purifies, and consecrates (John 17:17). You do not fight the devil on his terms of lies or anything contrary to the Word of God. You fight the devil on your God-given terms: holi-ness, purity, and truth of the Word! When you fight him on these premises, you can never lose because he has none of these things in him. He is not holy or pure. The devil cannot fight on the grounds of truth because there is no truth in him (John 8:44)."

> And the LORD God said unto the woman, What is this that thou hast done? And the woman said, The serpent beguiled me, and I did eat.
> —GENESIS 3:13

> But I fear, lest by any means, as the serpent beguiled Eve through his subtilty, so your minds should be corrupted from the simplicity that is in Christ.
> —2 CORINTHIANS 11:3

Satan has access to you to the degree that you agree with his words. Whatever you agree with him about, you give him access to. Satan rules by deceit. If you do not give Satan attention, he will not give you direction. You need to walk and live in the truth of the Word. It is only in this state that you can fight to win. You are not just throwing blows in the air, but you are fighting to win. A soldier should not go to the battlefield doubting if he will win. He cannot risk having this mindset because he knows that if he does not win, he may die on the battlefield or be taken captive. That is why the soldier has to be in boot camp and trained before going to the battlefield. It is a training of the mind and body. The soldier goes to the battlefield with a sound mind and a purposed heart that he will come back home victorious.

The loins are not only an anatomical position of the waist, but also the seat of procreative power. Just as an ordinary belt harnesses the waist, the belt of truth harnesses your procreative power. You go into battle with your procreative power harnessed with the truth of the Word of God. You have got to know that the procreative power of the Word of God is alive in you. You have got to know that the Word of God you speak shall come to pass; otherwise, you will be crippled with fear during warfare.

In the middle section of the front of a Roman soldier's belt, called the *cinculum militaire*, were strategically positioned hanging leather strips which were metal-studded and sometimes also had metal rings at their ends. These protected the most vulnerable part of the body—the sexual organs. The magnitude of truth is able to cover you completely as it reaches unto the clouds (Ps. 57:10) and endures to all generations (Ps. 100:5). The belt of truth causes you to walk in integrity. Integrity is a virtue that the devil has no part of. You cannot enter battle defiled because by so doing, you are entering in on the devil's terms instead of God's terms, and you can never win.

> For this is the will of God, that you should be con-
> secrated (separated and set apart for pure and holy
> living): that you should abstain and shrink from all
> sexual vice, that each one of you should know how
> to possess (control, manage) his own body in conse-
> cration (purity, separated from things profane), and
> honor, not [to be used] in the passion of lust like the
> heathen, who are ignorant of the true God and have
> no knowledge of His will.
>
> —1 THESSALONIANS 4:3–5, AMP

During counseling sessions, I have heard believers who
have willingly indulged in sexual sin say such things as,
"Pastor, I just do not know what happened." My response
is, "Were you sedated?" The Lord has given us power to
bring all our thoughts into captivity to the obedience of
Jesus Christ (2 Cor. 10:5) because sin first starts in the
mind. When you dwell long enough on thoughts about
sexual sin, they will lead you to the act.

> And behold, there met him a woman, dressed as a
> harlot and sly and cunning of heart.... With much
> justifying and enticing argument she persuades him,
> with the allurements of her lips she leads him [to
> overcome his conscience and his fears] and forces
> him along. Suddenly he [yields and] follows her
> reluctantly like an ox moving to the slaughter, like
> one in fetters going to the correction [to be given] to
> a fool or like a dog enticed by food to the muzzle till
> a dart [of passion] pierces and inflames his vitals;
> then like a bird fluttering straight into the net [he
> hastens], not knowing that it will cost him his life.
> Listen to me now therefore, O you sons, and be

attentive to the words of my mouth. Let not your heart incline toward her ways, do not stray into her paths. For she has cast down many wounded; indeed, all her slain are a mighty host.

—PROVERBS 7:10, 21–26, AMP

Many men and women of God have been taken out of ministry due to sexual sin. The Bible tells us that the strongest man ever, Samson, and the greatest king ever, David, were all victims of sexual sin. There is therefore a need for caution on everyone's part. Your sexual life has to be in order; otherwise, it will destroy the witness of Christ in you, and this is what the devil wants. God has called us to holiness as He is holy.

> For I am the LORD that bringeth you up out of the land of Egypt, to be your God: ye shall therefore be holy, for I am holy.
>
> —LEVITICUS 11:45

> And ye shall be holy unto me: for I the LORD am holy, and have severed you from other people, that ye should be mine.
>
> —LEVITICUS 20:26

> And that ye put on the new man, which after God is created in righteousness and true holiness.
>
> —EPHESIANS 4:24

> For ye know what commandments we gave you by the Lord Jesus. For this is the will of God, even your sanctification, that ye should abstain from forni-cation: That every one of you should know how to possess his vessel in sanctification and honour; not

in the lust of concupiscence, even as the Gentiles
which know not God: For God hath not called us
unto uncleanness, but unto holiness.

—1 THESSALONIANS 4:2–5, 7

That which was consecrated to God was used only for
Him and for none other. Being consecrated unto God
means that you are set apart unto Him alone. You are
not yours, but His! Everything in your life emanates from
and ends with Him because that which is consecrated
belongs to Him. The instruments that were in the tabernacle belonged to God. They did not belong to those God
told to make the instruments, but to the One who commissioned them; and the instruments were used only in
the service of God. They were not used part time in the
world. Do you not know that you are meant only for Him?
He does not have part ownership of you but whole ownership. As He sends you into the world to do His work, you
do not own the work, but He does. You are not to become
as the world. You are not to become as the ones you are
preaching to, but you are to lead them to Christ. You do
not belong to the world, but you belong to Him. He is the
One that leads you into what He has called you to with all
provision in place, and He is the One who leads you back
home (John 10:9). Never lose sight of the One to whom
you belong. It is only in doing God's will that you will
find satisfaction and joy because the will of God profits
much. God's provision and abundance is found in His will
because He satisfies His good pleasure (2 Thess. 1:11). The
will of God is in alignment with the heavenly mission.

Attached to the *cinculum militaire* was a sheath with a
Roman *pugio* dagger, a short two-edged blade which was
a stabbing weapon and the last line of defense in extreme

close-quarters combat. It was also used as a utility knife. Carried in a scabbard suspended from a shoulder belt and hooked into the *cinculum militaire* was the *gladius*, a close combat stabbing sword designed for stabbing and thrusting, rather than slashing. It had a 20 to 22-inch long two-edged blade that tapered to a sharp point, and its girth enabled tremendous shearing blows. In spiritual warfare, you do not just tap on the devil with your finger, but you tear him down. You are to pull down strongholds that have been erected against you (2 Cor. 10:4).

The *pugio* and *gladius* were attached to each side of the *cinculum militaire*. The belt of truth keeps everything in place and proper perspective. It frees the soldier's hands to hold the shield of faith and the sword of the Spirit. The Lord teaches your hands to war and your fingers to fight (Ps. 144:1). Slackness has no place in the life of a believer. Slackness is an inability to fully grasp what God has given you which results in grappling to hold onto what you know belongs to you. You cannot be effective or go forward if you are slack. You are also not able to lay hold of opportunities that God brings your way when you are slack. Sometimes there is a war cry in the heavenlies and the Lord is calling you to war in your spirit, but because your spirit is not resonating with the Spirit of the Lord, you want to sleep; you want to slack off. Pray that your spirit resonates with the Spirit of the Lord because you are created after His likeness and in His image. When this happens, you do not lag behind and there is no striving, but you are in synchronous movement and in tune with the Holy Spirit. Your spirit has free will to follow the Spirit of God. You are not bound in your spirit, for where the Spirit of God is, there is liberty. You are able to go God's way, understand when the Spirit of God speaks to you, and be quick in learning. Jesus was quick in learning because His Spirit moved with the Spirit of His Father. Declare divine ability to move in the things of God and in your calling. Take possession of the territory that God has given you. He is Lord of lords and King of kings and has given you territory to take over in which you rule and reign.

When one loosens or removes his belt, his pants can easily be removed or fall down, and what is meant to be private is now indecently exposed and leads to shame. Truth upholds and never makes ashamed. Every revelation of truth gives you the ability to firmly tighten the belt of truth around your waist, keeping everything in place so that it cannot be ripped off! It is the truth you know that makes you free from being slave to sin (John 8:32), gives you supremacy over Satan in battle, and enables you to do exploits for God (Dan. 11:32). When Jesus was tempted, He used the truth of the Word and Satan had to flee for a season. Satan also quoted the Word, but he did so out of context and twisted it.

Jesus' Spirit is the Spirit of truth. John 16:13 tells us that the Holy Spirit guides us into all truth. The truth of the Word tells us that we have not received from God the spirit of bondage again to fear (Rom. 8:15). It is Satan who gives the spirit of bondage to fear, and so we refuse fear. As a result, we do not enter battle with fear, doubt, or premonition because we have received from God the spirit of power (*dunamis*), love (*agape*), and a sound mind (self-discipline or self-control) (2 Tim. 1:7). Everything you acquire through compromise of the truth of the Word of God, you will lose. Everything you acquire through standing and continuing in the truth of the Word of God will give you eternal value.

If you do not get out of the Word of God, you will not be ensnared by the devil and his works.

The only way you can run the race in a manner that is acceptable to God and finish it is by surrendering every area of your life to Him. You cannot afford to leave any area of your life not surrendered to God as that is the area in which Satan will have legal right. Any area not surrendered is where Satan will have a hook in you, and you will not be able to finish the race. It is not only the ability to run the race that we should focus on, but also the need to finish it. This cannot be accomplished when there is a hook in your spirit because each time you try to run forward, the hook the devil has in you will pull you back. That is why 2 Timothy 2:4 tells us that we should not be entangled with the things of this world because entanglement will pull us back.

Jesus is coming back for a church without blemish, spot, or wrinkle (Eph. 5:27), people in whose lives Satan has no hook. It is time we stopped struggling to follow Jesus. Our struggles are because of areas in our lives that are not surrendered to Him; the person who is fully surrendered is free to run. Have you ever seen a runner running a race with a rope around his waist that is tied to a stake? How can he run? Each time he attempts to move forward, he is pulled back with equal force. Declare this day where your commitment lies. Is it to God, or is it to the world? If you are committed to God, then you will not price anything in this world higher or greater than Him. God has given us everything in Jesus Christ to make us free to run. Who do you choose this day? Those who choose God are enabled by Him to run the race. Where the Spirit of the Lord is, there is liberty (2 Cor. 3:17). Liberty to follow Him!

When a woman gets married, she does not tell her husband, "This part of my life I am keeping it to myself. This other part you can have." Any woman that does that will not allow her marriage to succeed. You have to give your all and trust God. He is a good God; He is not man, and He is not out to trick you. He is not out to ruin you. He loves you with an everlasting love. You need to tell Him, "Lord, I am available to you. Help me to release all areas of my life to You. I give You my all. I am no longer going to be my own protector. I am no longer going to be my own keeper. I am no longer going to be my own enabler. I am going to allow You to do all things in my life. Your desire is my desire. I give You my thoughts, O Lord God, and You will order my ways aright. I give You my children. I give You my spouse. I give You everything that pertains to me. All my worldly possessions I give to You, Lord God. Nothing is going to hold me bound on this Earth. Nothing is going to hold me from giving my life to You. Everything about me I give to You. My service in the ministry I give to You because You are above ministry. You are above all. I wake up giving all to You. I go to bed giving all to You, Lord God."

It is in our giving our all to God that we give Him glory. Jesus said that the Son of man has nowhere to lay His head because every day of His life, He gave it to God. It was always, "My Father, what would You have Me do?" Jesus always said what He heard His Father say because He was always after God's will, and He gave Him His all (John 5:30). At the end of the day, He said, "Lord, My Father, everything that You asked Me to do, I have done it. Glorify Me" (see John 17:4–5).

> Who can say, I have made my heart clean, I am pure
> from my sin?
>   —Proverbs 20:9

You cannot on your own or of your self-will make your heart clean and pure. You cannot trust yourself to have clean hands. You cannot trust yourself not to speak falsehood nor trust your eyes not to see evil. You can only do all of this through total, absolute, and complete surrender to God through the Holy Spirit.

When we serve in the church, we should give God our all. It does not matter whether we are commended or not. We give Him our all because that's what He deserves. When you give yourself to God, you need to give Him everything—your time, love, faithfulness, finances, plans, ambitions, family, job—you give everything! You lay everything down before Him—all that you are. It is when you give yourself to Him that He can use you, because the Lord will not share you with anyone or anything. You might be saying, "No. This particular area of my life is my business, Lord; You cannot step in. In this particular area of my life, I will do things the way I want—but this other part I will do things according to Your will." The Lord says, "No. I have to have it all." It is when you give yourself to Him that Satan's shackles fall off you because the shackles cannot remain in the place of obedience. Captivity cannot remain in the place of obedience. Yokes cannot remain in the place of obedience. Burdens have to fall off in the place of obedience. God is your keeper. You were not structured or created to keep yourself. God did not say, "Adam, keep yourself." He said, "Keep the garden." However, some of us try to keep ourselves and we fail so awfully, but I pray that you have the heart to give yourself to the Lord.

Start asking the Lord now to show you areas of your life that are not surrendered to Him from the smallest to the biggest. You do not want the devil to have any hook in you, even as Jesus said that the devil has nothing in Him. Jesus could only go to the cross because the devil had nothing in Him! The only way we can fully accomplish God's will is when the devil has nothing in us because we belong wholly to God! God has not called us in part, but in whole. That which enters God's kingdom is whole, and it is He that makes whole. This is a time of sanctification of the church of Christ, but will we stand to be sanctified? Those who belong to Him, He sanctifies. Ask the Holy Spirit to help you run undefiled without any hook in you that attaches you to the world—free in Christ so that your life will give glory to God.

> But he that doeth truth cometh to the light, that his deeds may be made manifest, that they are wrought in God.
>
> —JOHN 3:21

You are to "do" truth on a continual basis, just as Jesus did, and thereby come to and walk in the light of God. When you do truth, everything you do is done in God.

> Into thine hand I commit my spirit: thou hast redeemed me, O LORD God of truth.
>
> —PSALM 31:5

You can only operate in the likeness of God if you are in God. God created us to do everything "in Him," not outside Him. In John 3:21, the Greek word *en* (English, "in") means a fixed position in. We are not to be vacillating in and out of God, but we are to operate from a fixed position in Him through Christ. The only competence by which Jesus could operate was to do things in the same manner He saw His Father do and say what He heard His Father say. God's Word cannot fail—because God can never fail! He decides what is good for your soul. What we ask God is usually for our now, but that which He gives is not only for our now but also for our future. That which He gives is in consonance with His purpose and His will for our lives. It is in line with His plan for creation. Will you, the created thing, question the Creator of all things?

We become deviant by doing things outside God. God created us to operate in Him. That is why He asked Adam in the Garden of Eden, "Where are you?" Is it that God did not know where Adam was? No, but God knew that Adam was now operating outside Him in spirit. God made all the trees pleasant to the sight and good for food including the tree of the knowledge of good and evil (Gen. 2:9). However, that was not supposed to be Adam and Eve's source of wisdom. Their source of all things was supposed to be God, and if they desired wisdom, they were to ask God who would give them liberally without upbraiding them (James 1:5).

Adam and Eve sought wisdom from the tree of the knowledge of good and evil which was outside God. That was deviant. As the new creation, the only way to operate is "in Him" and for Him, which is how God originally designed man to live in the Garden of Eden. That is how the voice of the world will become silent to you. You should only allow the Holy Spirit to speak into your life, and you should only receive godly counsel. You should listen every day to what the Word of God is going to speak to your heart. There is no other way you can live. You cannot live outside God, and you do not want to live outside Him, for there is no life outside Him.

> Seeing ye have purified your souls in obeying the truth through the Spirit unto unfeigned love of the brethren, see that ye love one another with a pure heart fervently.
> —1 PETER 1:22

Obedience to truth through enablement of the Holy Spirit purifies your heart and soul to unfeigned love for the brethren. We have to learn to walk in unfeigned and fervent love with our brothers and sisters in Christ.

> He that saith he is in the light, and hateth his brother, is in darkness even until now. He that loveth his brother abideth in the light, and there is none occasion of stumbling in him. But he that hateth his brother is in darkness, and walketh in darkness, and knoweth not whither he goeth, because that darkness hath blinded his eyes.
> —1 JOHN 2:9–11

It is only when there is unity amongst believers that we can walk corporately in the light of God and win battles as the body of Christ. The devil knows this, and that is why he brings division and disaffection amongst the brethren.

> Behold, how good and how pleasant it is for brethren to dwell together in unity! It is like the precious ointment upon the head, that ran down upon the beard, even Aaron's beard: that went down to the skirts of his garments; as the dew of Hermon, and as the dew that descended upon the mountains of

Zion: for there the LORD commanded the blessing,
even life for evermore.
—PSALM 133:1–3

You want to live in the congregation of the living because
He is God of the living and not of the dead. Seven days a
week—live for Him. Morning, afternoon, and evening you
are to live for Him. Living for God becomes your lifestyle.
Whatever situation you are in, you must live for God. The
world tells us to live for ourselves, but God's Word says
we should live for Him. The created thing lives for the
Creator. We cannot use the world's standard because it is
enmity to God. It is a lie, and it will take you to hell. Live
for God. Even in places you feel alone, live for God. We
must go to God first in everything—this is the wiring of
the new creation. Anything and any place outside God is
darkness because God is light.

> This then is the message which we have heard of
> him, and declare unto you, that God is light, and in
> him is no darkness at all.
> —1 JOHN 1:5

ENDNOTES

1. *American Heritage Dictionary of the English Language,* 5th ed., s.v., "true."
2. *Pseudologos,* "speaking falsely," Strong's G5573.
3. *Menó,* "continue," Strong's G3306.
4. *Ginóskó,* "know," Strong's G1097.
5. *Perizónnumi,* "girt about," Strong's G4024.

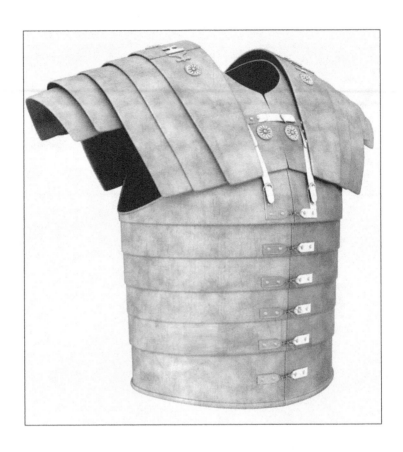

Chapter 3

BREASTPLATE *of* RIGHTEOUSNESS

Stand therefore, having your loins
girt about with truth, and having on
the breastplate of righteousness
—Ephesians 6:14

I N THIS CHAPTER, you will learn about the place righteousness has in spiritual warfare. What is the meaning of righteousness? Righteousness is a state of being in right standing with God. This is the state every believer should be in on a daily basis. It is only when you are in right standing with God that you have one hundred percent victory. Jesus' righteousness sustained Him, and righteousness is His breastplate (Isa. 59:16–17). God's righteousness is our weapon in fighting our enemies—not our self righteousness. Self righteousness is as filthy rags in the sight of God (Isa. 64:6). It is the truth of the Word of God that you know, understand, or perceive that causes you to respond to situations in ways that are right in the sight of God; therefore, you can put on the breastplate of righteousness. Believing and doing God's Word is righteousness in God's sight (Rom. 4:3).

> For it is not those who hear the law who are righteous in God's sight, but it is those who obey the law who will be declared righteous.
>
> —ROMANS 2:13, NIV

Keep the Word of God in the center of your heart and not at the periphery as an add-on after you have filled your heart with other things. The commanded Word of God is to be in your heart (Deut. 6:6). When the Word of God is at the periphery of your heart, it can easily be pushed out when situations arise, but when it is at the center, it becomes engrafted. An engraftment is an implant. To engraft means to plant or introduce something foreign deeply and firmly into that which is native for the purpose of propagation to continue or multiply that kind by generation or successive production. An engraftment takes over the thing that it is engrafted into and thrives, restoring health and allowing it have a normal life as ordained by God. So, it is not how much Word you have in you that matters, but how much engrafted Word that is in you. It is the engrafted or implanted Word of God that is able to save your soul (James 1:21). The word *save* in Greek is *sózó* which means save, deliver, protect, heal, preserve, or make whole.[1] It is the engrafted Word of God in your heart that is life to you and health to all your flesh (Prov. 4:22).

What makes the Word of God an engraftment? Meditating on it! Meditating is not just reading the Word, but seeing yourself in the Word and applying it to your daily life. It entails devoting time to the Word, asking the Holy Spirit to teach and reveal the Word to you, doing

Word studies, and cross referencing the Word using a Bible concordance and other tools available to you. You should go over the Word again and again till your spirit receives it and you live it. Meditating means eating and digesting the Word so that you become one with it and unable to deviate from it. Meditating causes logos to become rhéma. It is only the revealed Word of God that can penetrate the center of one's heart and become engrafted. It is only when you have the Word of God richly in your heart that you can speak it because from the abundance of the heart, the mouth speaks (Matt. 12:34).

> Of his own will begat he us with the word of truth, that we should be a kind of firstfruits of his creatures. Wherefore, my beloved brethren, let every man be swift to hear, slow to speak, slow to wrath: for the wrath of man worketh not the righteousness of God. Wherefore lay apart all filthiness and superfluity of naughtiness, and receive with meekness the engrafted word, which is able to save your souls.
> —JAMES 1:18–21

There are people who know the Bible from Genesis to Revelation, but their lives remain all bound up because they only have head knowledge of the Word. The Word has not been engrafted in their hearts because they are devoid of the spirit of meekness. Meekness is the disposition to be gentle, kind, steadfast, and patient in suffering injuries without feeling a spirit of revenge because you trust in God and fear Him. Meekness is being completely submitted to God's Word. It emanates from the Holy Spirit and is a fruit of the Spirit. This is how Jesus described Himself in Matthew 11:29. Without meekness, you cannot receive the engrafted Word of God.

In the Roman Empire, when there was a decisive victory at war that brought the war to an end with no less than 5000 of the enemy's army slain, the Roman captain of the winning army would be granted a triumph. He would come forth in a royal chariot dressed in beautiful apparel, wearing a crown, and publicly displaying all his captives in chains as well as the seized weaponry of the enemy. This is what Jesus Christ did on the cross of Calvary over 2000 years ago. He made a public show of principalities and powers and all the weaponry of the devil (Col. 2:15). This is why you do not need to be afraid. All you need to do is to obey the Word of God. In the Roman Empire, for a leader to have a triumph on the streets of Rome, he could not just be a captain of a battalion; he needed to come from the royal family or be an emperor. You are royalty. Believers are a royal priesthood because Jesus has made us kings and priests unto God (Rev. 1:6; 5:10). As king, it is your right to triumph. Triumph is beyond victory. It is only a special class of people that can triumph, and Jesus Christ has placed you in this class (2 Cor. 2:14). God always causes you to triumph in Christ Jesus.

God has seated believers in heavenly places in Christ Jesus; therefore, your place of seating is above all principalities, all powers, and all dominion (Eph. 2:6). It is in this place of divine sitting that God has blessed us with all spiritual blessings (Eph. 1:3). This is why you can always triumph in Christ. Whatever you might be going through, you need to start saying to yourself, "I will triumph." A triumph was a public display that the whole city came out to see. When the Lord brings you out of your circumstance, it will be public testimony to the goodness and might of our God.

There were two types of breastplate worn by the Roman soldier.

- The *lorica hamata* was worn by the *auxilia* who were the light troops. This was a mail of bronze or iron concentric rings which were interlocking. An arrow could go through one of its rings. However, the Lord has not called us to be light troops. He has called us to be heavily armed soldiers.

- The *lorica segmentata* was worn by heavily armed soldiers, and it was segmented armor in two parts. It was made up of iron strips fastened to internal leather straps and arranged horizontally, overlapping downward and surrounding the torso in two halves, fastened in the front and back. The overlapping strips had no space between them which made the *lorica segmentata* more protective than the *lorica hamata*. The upper body and shoulders were protected by additional strips or shoulder guards. The shoulder strips extended to the proximal part of the arm. There were breast and back plates to cover the front and back of the thorax. The fitments that closed the various plate sections together were buckles, lobate hinges, hinged straps, tie hooks, tie rings, etc., and were made of brass.

The *lorica segmentata* is the piece referred to as the breastplate of righteousness. In the Old Testament, the high priest had a breastplate of judgment which was double (Exod. 39:9) and tied up at the front and at the back. I have heard people say such things as, "I have got your back because the armor of God is exposed at the back." This is completely wrong. Whatever God does is complete. The whole armor of God is complete for our protection.

> And he saw that there was no man, and wondered that there was no intercessor: therefore his arm brought salvation unto him; and his righteousness, it sustained him. For he put on righteousness as a breastplate, and an helmet of salvation upon his head; and he put on the garments of vengeance for clothing, and was clad with zeal as a cloak.
>
> —ISAIAH 59:16–17

From this scripture, we see that the work of Jesus Christ on the cross was intercession on our behalf for our redemption from sin. In this warfare, His righteousness sustained Him as He put it on as a breastplate. Jesus put on the armor of God to accomplish the work of salvation. In Isaiah 53:11, Jesus is called God's righteous servant who justifies many! He is Jehovah Tsidkenu; God our Righteousness. Isaiah 64:6 says that we are all unclean and that all our righteousness is as filthy rags before God. However, there is good news—we are made the righteousness of God in Christ Jesus (2 Cor. 5:21). This is imputed righteousness. In warfare, it is God's righteousness, i.e., imputed righteousness through Jesus Christ that sustains us, bears us up, takes hold of us, and props us. Jesus judges and makes war in righteousness (Rev. 19:11). So should we! Everything we do should be in righteousness as we are the righteousness of God in Christ Jesus. What is important in warfare is not necessarily what the enemy is doing, but more importantly, what our response is. Is our response right before God? Is our response in line with God's Word? What the enemy is doing is a mere distraction from our Christian walk. Operating in God's righteousness protects our heart from taking offence, being wounded, and wanting to take revenge. It prevents your lungs from taking in the foul air of negative words spoken to you. Instead, choose to love always. Love covers all sins (Prov. 10:12).

> Being justified freely by his grace through the redemption that is in Christ Jesus: whom God hath set forth [to be] a propitiation through faith in his blood, to declare his righteousness for the remission of sins that are past, through the forbearance of God; to declare, I say, at this time his righteousness: that he might be just, and the justifier of him which believeth in Jesus.
> —ROMANS 3:24–26

Christ's righteousness is declared over us through His blood for the remission of our past sins (Rom. 3:25). The breastplate of righteousness declares that Christ is your justifier. You enter battle not accused, not condemned, but justified by Jesus Christ and knowing that you are the righteousness of God in Him. Have you ever seen a general on the battlefield asking the recruits whether they should fight or hide? In battle, the junior officers look to the general for instructions about which way they should go, and when they see the boldness he exhibits, they are encouraged and say, "We can do this. We can win. We

can defeat the enemy!" No soldier wants to be led by a
general who is shivering and shaking with fear on the
battlefield because he knows that following such a leader
leads to defeat. You cannot enter battle in doubt and unbelief, not knowing who you are in Christ Jesus, and then
expect to win. You enter into battle confident of what
Jesus Christ has done for you. It does not matter how filthy
your past sins were. The important question is, "Have you
repented of them and received Jesus Christ as your Lord
and Savior?" If you have, then you have been justified. It
does not matter whether people are still talking about the
"old you." You know that your old man is dead in Christ
Jesus. Romans 4:25 says that Jesus was delivered for our
offences or sins and raised again for our justification. The
word *justification* means the establishment of a person as
just by acquittal from guilt, a concrete expression of righteousness.[2] Acts 13:10 tells us that the devil and his cohorts
are enemies of all righteousness. The devil is the accuser
of the brethren. You have to rise up and say, "I am the
righteousness of God through Jesus Christ. I have been
justified by Jesus Christ!" You lock into God by locking
into His Word.

> For in the Gospel a righteousness which God
> ascribes is revealed, both springing from faith and
> leading to faith [disclosed through the way of faith
> that arouses to more faith]. As it is written, The man
> who through faith is just and upright shall live and
> shall live by faith.
>
> —ROMANS 1:17, AMP

This righteousness is not by works (Rom. 4:6). It is God's righteousness, which springs from having faith in Jesus Christ, and it leads to more faith and no fear.

> And not as it was by one that sinned, so is the gift: for the judgment was by one to condemnation, but the free gift is of many offences unto justification. For if by one man's offence death reigned by one; much more they which receive abundance of grace and of the gift of righteousness shall reign in life by one, Jesus Christ.) Therefore as by the offence of one judgment came upon all men to condemnation; even so by the righteousness of one the free gift came upon all men unto justification of life. For as by one man's disobedience many were made sinners, so by the obedience of one shall many be made righteous. Moreover the law entered, that the offence might abound. But where sin abounded, grace did much more abound: That as sin hath reigned unto death, even so might grace reign through righteousness unto eternal life by Jesus Christ our Lord.
> —ROMANS 5:16–21

The summary of Romans 5:16–21 is as follows:

- Through one man (Adam) → Sin entered the world → Death entered through sin.

- Through one man (Jesus) → Abundance of grace reigns → Gift of righteousness through grace comes upon all.

THEREFORE

- By one man's offence (Adam) →
  Condemnation (judgment) entered

- By one man's righteousness (Jesus) →
  Justification (free gift of God) reigns

The components of the *lorica segmentata* had to be tied up and arranged in proper order, allowing no space in between the overlapping strips so that there would be no exposure of the protected area to the enemy's onslaught. It was tightly fitted to the body in this manner, adequately protecting the vital organs of the chest: the heart and lungs. A person is certified dead when his heart stops beating and he stops breathing. You are to guard your heart with all diligence, for out of it are the issues of life. Just as the breastplate strips were arranged, you need to arrange precept upon precept, line upon line of the Word of God (Isa. 28:10) in your walk of obedience with no jot or tittle removed (Matt. 5:18).

The Greek word for *obedience* is *hupakoe* from *hupo* which means "under" and *akouo* which means "to hear." *Hupakoé* means attentive hearkening, compliance, or submission.[3] According to *Webster's Dictionary, obedience* means compliance with a command, prohibition, or known law and rule of duty prescribed; the performance of what is required or enjoined by authority; or the abstaining from what is prohibited, in compliance with the command or prohibition.[4] To constitute obedience, the act or forbearance to act must be in submission to authority; the command must be known to the person, and his compliance must be in consequence of it—or it is not obedience.

It is one thing to be saved. It is another thing to be obedient. God is calling believers to obedience. We get carried away with our different areas of service, positions in the church, and ministry. All God wants and requires of us is obedience. Are we born obedient? No. Obedience is learned in our Christian walk and not acquired by the laying on of hands or by impartation!

> Though he were a Son, yet learned he obedience by the things which he suffered; and being made perfect, he became the author of eternal salvation unto all them that obey him.
> —HEBREWS 5:8–9

Even though Jesus is the Son of God, while on Earth, He learned obedience from the things He experienced. Your walk is perfect or complete when you walk in obedience to God, and obedience always yields its fruit. It therefore means that if you walk outside God's will and command, your walk is imperfect in God's sight. The walk of obedience is the walk that is blessed. In Genesis 17:1–2, let us see what God told Abraham:

> And when Abram was ninety years old and nine, the LORD appeared to Abram, and said unto him, I am the Almighty God; walk before me, and be thou perfect. And I will make my covenant between me and thee, and will multiply thee exceedingly.

God is perfect (Matt. 5:48); His work is perfect (Deut. 32:4); His law is perfect (Ps. 19:7); and His way is perfect (2 Sam. 22:31).

> Be ye therefore perfect, even as your Father which is
> in heaven is perfect.
> —MATTHEW 5:48

Let us see what God says about Satan in Ezekiel 28:15, 17:

> Thou wast perfect in thy ways from the day that thou
> wast created, till iniquity was found in thee.... Thine
> heart was lifted up because of thy beauty, thou hast
> corrupted thy wisdom by reason of thy brightness:
> I will cast thee to the ground, I will lay thee before
> kings, that they may behold thee.

When a heart lacks obedience, it cultivates pride.

> Establish my steps and direct them by [means of]
> Your word; let not any iniquity have dominion
> over me.
> —PSALM 119:133, AMP

OBEDIENCE TO GOD
AS FAMILY HEADS

As a result of Noah's obedience, God revealed:

1. His plan for the destruction of man, every
   living thing, and the Earth to Noah (Gen.
   6:13). Revelation of God's plan for our nations
   can be gotten through obedience.

2. His strategy for Noah's family's safety and
   deliverance.

In obedience, Noah built the ark according to God's
command. He did not say, "Let me use another type of

wood." When you do exactly what God says, what you build endures the storms of life and overcomes the devices and schemes of Satan.

As a family head, your obedience to God plays a vital role in the preservation of your family from destruction, spiritually and physically. After building the ark, Noah waited for God's instruction to go into the ark with his family (Gen. 7:1). Because he waited for God's command, when they entered the ark, God shut the door. When we walk in the timing of God, He brings us into what He has for us and shuts the door behind us so that the devourer cannot come in to get us or our family members. The door that God shuts, no man can open (Rev. 3:7). The result was the preservation of Noah's family, as well as the animals and birds he brought into the ark. He built a hedge around them through obedience to God and now became the father of a new generation.

Even after Noah knew that the waters had abated and the earth was dry, he waited on God to tell him to go out of the ark (Gen. 8:16). So, when he came out with his entire household, he was able to offer unto God a sweet-smelling sacrifice. As a result, God came into covenant with Noah and his family (which now constituted all humankind) and the Earth. As a family head, do you acknowledge God in the coming in and going out of your family daily? Acknowledge Him by calling upon His name in prayer and walking in obedience to His Word.

Obedience in God's Service

God told Moses to build a tabernacle where He would dwell and meet with His people. This was something that had never been done before. In Exodus chapters 25 to 31, we read God's instructions to Moses about:

1. The materials to be used in the building of the tabernacle as well as the instruments to be used.

2. The workers to be recruited—workers whom God had filled with the Spirit of God in wisdom, understanding, and knowledge in all manner of workmanship.

3. Commands about the priesthood

4. Offerings and Sabbath

In Exodus chapters 36 to 40, Moses carried out God's instructions. He did not try to modify what God had said should be done by using his own human wisdom. He just obeyed. If you read what Moses did, it is a mirror image of what God told him to do.

> Thus did Moses: according to all that the LORD com-manded him, so did he.
> —EXODUS 40:16

Moses finished the work of the tabernacle, and then a cloud covered the tent of the congregation, and the glory of the Lord filled the tabernacle (Exod. 40:33–34). When we carry out God's instructions and commands to the last letter, then it is acceptable and pleasing in His sight and the glory of God will be seen in it. If a book were to be written about God's commands to you and what you have done or are doing, what would it look like? Would the chapters about what you have done or are doing be a mirror image of God's instructions to you? Obedience is not just doing what God has asked you to do, but doing it in God's specified way.

This is what God said about Samuel in 1 Samuel 2:35:

> And I will raise me up a faithful priest, that shall do according to that which is in mine heart and in my mind: and I will build him a sure house; and he shall walk before mine anointed for ever.

OBEDIENCE IN YOUR CALLING

And thou, Solomon my son, know thou the God of thy father, and serve him with a perfect heart and with a willing mind: for the LORD searcheth all hearts, and understandeth all the imaginations of the thoughts: if thou seek him, he will be found of thee; but if thou forsake him, he will cast thee off for ever. Take heed now; for the LORD hath chosen thee to build an house for the sanctuary: be strong, and do it. Then David gave to Solomon his son the pattern of the porch, and of the houses thereof, and of the treasuries thereof, and of the upper chambers thereof, and of the inner parlours thereof, and of the place of the mercy seat, And the pattern of all that he had by the spirit, of the courts of the house of the LORD, and of all the chambers round about, of the treasuries of the house of God, and of the treasuries of the dedicated things: Also for the courses of the priests and the Levites, and for all the work of the service of the house of the LORD, and for all the vessels of service in the house of the LORD.

—1 CHRONICLES 28:9–13

BUT

For it came to pass, when Solomon was old, that his wives turned away his heart after other gods: and his heart was not perfect with the LORD his God, as was the heart of David his father. And Solomon did evil in the sight of the LORD, and went not fully after the LORD, as did David his father. And the LORD was angry with Solomon, because his heart was turned from the LORD God of Israel, which had appeared unto him twice, and had commanded him concerning this thing, that he should not go after other gods: but he kept not that which the LORD commanded.

—1 KINGS 11:4, 6, 9–10

We are to obey God till the very end of our days.

OBEDIENCE IN LEADERSHIP

And Saul said unto Samuel, Yea, I have obeyed the voice of the LORD, and have gone the way which the LORD sent me, and have brought Agag the king of Amalek, and have utterly destroyed the Amalekites. But the people took of the spoil, sheep and oxen, the chief of the things which should have been utterly destroyed, to sacrifice unto the LORD thy God in Gilgal. And Samuel said, Hath the LORD as great delight in burnt offerings and sacrifices, as in obeying the voice of the LORD? Behold, to obey is better than sacrifice, and to hearken than the fat of rams. For rebellion is as the sin of witchcraft, and stubbornness is as iniquity and idolatry. Because thou hast rejected the word of the LORD, he hath also rejected thee from being king. And Saul said unto Samuel, I have sinned: for I have transgressed the commandment of the LORD, and thy words: because I feared the people, and obeyed their voice.

—1 SAMUEL 15:20–24

As a leader appointed by God, when the word of the people under you is different from the Word of the Lord, you do the Word of the Lord. The people did not set you up as leader and do not have the power to do so. God did, and you take your instructions from God and not from the people. The fear of God goes hand in hand with obedience to Him.

The LORD commanded us to obey all these decrees and to fear the LORD our God, so that we might always prosper and be kept alive, as is the case today.

—DEUTERONOMY 6:24, NIV

The fear of the Lord is the beginning of knowledge and wisdom (Prov. 1:7; 9:10).

Benefits of the fear of God are:

Provision

O fear the LORD, ye his saints: for there is no want to them that fear him.

—PSALM 34:9

Deliverance

> But the LORD your God ye shall fear; and he shall
> deliver you out of the hand of all your enemies.
> —2 KINGS 17:39

> He will fulfil the desire of them that fear him: he
> also will hear their cry, and will save them.
> —PSALM 145:19

Long, Fulfilled Life

> The fear of the LORD prolongeth days: but the years
> of the wicked shall be shortened.
> —PROVERBS 10:27

Blessing on You and Your Family

> Blessed is every one that feareth the LORD; that
> walketh in his ways. For thou shalt eat the labour
> of thine hands: happy shalt thou be, and it shall be
> well with thee. Thy wife shall be as a fruitful vine
> by the sides of thine house: thy children like olive
> plants round about thy table. Behold, that thus
> shall the man be blessed that feareth the LORD. The
> LORD shall bless thee out of Zion: and thou shalt
> see the good of Jerusalem all the days of thy life.
> Yea, thou shalt see thy children's children, and
> peace upon Israel.
> —PSALM 128

Prosperity

> Praise ye the LORD. Blessed is the man that
> feareth the LORD, that delighteth greatly in his

commandments. Wealth and riches shall be in his
house: and his righteousness endureth for ever.

—PSALM 112:1, 3

God's Everlasting Mercy

And his mercy is on them that fear him from generation to generation.

—LUKE 1:50

God's Guidance and Peace

What man is he that feareth the LORD? him shall he
teach in the way that he shall choose. His soul shall
dwell at ease; and his seed shall inherit the earth.

—PSALM 25:12–13

Revelation of God's Secrets

The secret of the LORD is with them that fear him;
and he will shew them his covenant.

—PSALM 25:14

Healing

Be not wise in thine own eyes: fear the LORD, and
depart from evil. It shall be health to thy navel, and
marrow to thy bones.

—PROVERBS 3:7–8

God's Protection

Ye that fear the LORD, trust in the LORD: he is their
help and their shield.

—PSALM 115:11

The high priest's breastplate bore the names of the tribes of Israel, and in it were put the Urim and Thummim. The high priest was to bear the judgment of the children of Israel upon his heart before the Lord continually (Exod. 28:29–30). *Urim* means lights and *Thummim* means perfections—complete truth.[5] God is the Father of lights (James 1:17). Jesus is the light of the world (John 8:12); His life is the light of men (John 1:4); and He is the truth (John 14:6). Each believer is the light of the world (Matt. 5:14).

In this dispensation, God has given believers His breastplate of righteousness and not judgment. All the law is fulfilled in Jesus who is the end of the law for righteousness to all who believe (Rom. 10:4). The scepter of righteousness is the scepter of God's kingdom (Heb. 1:8). God's kingdom is righteousness, peace, and joy in the Holy Ghost (Rom. 14:17).

God's righteousness:

- Is eternal (Ps. 119:142)

- Delivers from death (Prov. 11:4)

- Directs and keeps the upright in the way (Prov. 11:5; 13:6)

- Exalts a nation (Prov. 14:34)

- Quickens the spirit (Rom. 8:10)

The ministration of righteousness exceeds in glory more than the ministration of condemnation (2 Cor. 3:9). Believers need to continually operate in God's righteousness. If we do this as the body of Christ, there will be exceeding glory in the church. Sometimes we move out of our place because we are more conscious of our former sinful state than our present righteous state. We need to repent of such instances because the blood of Jesus wrought righteousness on our behalf.

You should not allow the devil play with your mind and speak lies into your destiny, thereby giving you low self esteem. It is what the Word of God says you are that you are. You should no longer stand in guilt, shame, and condemnation, but in your righteous place in Christ. You are a blood-washed child of God. That is why God calls you His son. When you have perfect understanding of the Word of God, you will know who you are in Christ. Sons of God are not sinners but are the righteousness of God in Christ because as our Father is, that is how we are in this world (1 John 4:17). The Spirit of God lives and dwells in you. His Spirit is the Spirit of holiness, and the Lord God has called you unto holiness. Anything that comes against you comes against the righteousness and holiness of God.

We serve a God in whom there is no shadow of turning (James 1:17). When you come to Him, know that you are coming to a God in whom there is no error and who cannot make a mistake. You are coming to a God who cannot wrongly assess your situation, who is precise, exact, and knows all things. The problem is not in the issue at hand, but in our hearts. If you see God as your God, then you will also see Him as your provision. If you know Him as your provision, then there will not be any doubt in you that God will not be able to provide or do that which He has spoken. Over the centuries, God's name has remained I AM. You cannot use the past tense when referring to His name because His name is ever present. There is no

limitation in Him. The limitation is in your heart. God
brings you out from a tight place, and He places you in an
enlarged place. Who enlarges the place? God! The place of
enlargement that God puts you in is defined by the purpose and plan He has for your life. You might think that
you have reached your limit, but who says when it is your
limit? Is it you or is it God? Is there anything God has
said that He has not done? When we are told to bring God
into remembrance of what He has said, it is not because
He has forgotten; it is to bring that particular Word to the
foremost part of our minds. All you need to do this day
is to agree with God that He is who He says He is. Do
you know that your very countenance depicts whether
you believe God or not? This is because when He speaks
a Word and you believe it in your heart, you will rejoice
before the answer manifests because you know that God
can never miss the mark.

> For what saith the scripture? Abraham believed
> God, and it was counted unto him for righteousness.
> Now to him that worketh is the reward not reck-
> oned of grace, but of debt. But to him that worketh
> not, but believeth on him that justifieth the ungodly,
> his faith is counted for righteousness.
> —ROMANS 4:3–5

> And being not weak in faith, he considered not his
> own body now dead, when he was about an hun-
> dred years old, neither yet the deadness of Sara's
> womb: He staggered not at the promise of God
> through unbelief; but was strong in faith, giving
> glory to God; and being fully persuaded that, what
> he had promised, he was able also to perform. And

therefore it was imputed to him for righteousness. Now it was not written for his sake alone, that it was imputed to him; but for us also, to whom it shall be imputed, if we believe on him that raised up Jesus our Lord from the dead; who was delivered for our offences, and was raised again for our justification.

—ROMANS 4:19–25

When God created Adam, He created him in His image and in His likeness, and that means God created man not to miss the mark. So, when Adam named the animals and the fowls of the air, he never missed the mark. It is only when doubt came into his heart about God's Word and he sinned that he started missing the mark. God has redeemed this in us through His Son, Jesus Christ, so when you speak as the redeemed of the Lord, you speak as one who cannot miss the mark. Jesus Christ on the cross of Calvary did not miss the mark, and His Spirit resides in the believer. That is why the Word of God says that Jesus strengthens you to do all things. It means that in Christ you never miss the mark. You might be questioning in your spirit right now as you read these words and say, "Sometimes I miss the mark." You miss the mark because you are not Spirit led, because those who are led by the Spirit of Christ do not miss the mark.

The eyes of the LORD are upon the righteous, and his ears are open unto their cry.... The righteous cry, and the LORD heareth, and delivereth them out of all their troubles.

—PSALM 34:15, 17

Say,

I am the righteousness of God in Christ Jesus. The Lord has made me to sit in heavenly places in Christ Jesus, and I declare that I shall no longer vacate my heavenly seating in Christ. It is from this exalted position that I operate in victory and triumph. I speak to the waters before me; I say depart in the name of Jesus. I speak to the mountain before me; I say be gone into the sea in the name of Jesus. I speak to obstacles and hindrances; I say out of my way in the name of Jesus. I take authority in the spirit over everything that has come against me and the destiny and purpose of my life. I say be gone in Jesus' name because I go into warfare with the breastplate of righteousness on me. So devil, you can no longer mess up my health or the destiny and purpose for my life, in Jesus' name. Amen.

ENDNOTES

1. *Sózó*, "to save," Strong's G4982.

2. W. E. Vine, Merrill Unger, William White, *Vine's Complete Expository Dictionary, vol. 2* (Nashville, TN: T. Nelson, 1996), s.v., "justification," 284.

3. *Hupakoé*, "obedience," Strong's G5218; *Vine's Complete Expository Dictionary*, vol. 3, 123.

4. *Webster's American Dictionary*, s.v., "obedience," (1828).

5. *Urim* ("lights"), *Thummim* ("perfections"), Strong's H224, H8550.

Chapter 4

SHOES *of* PEACE

*And having shod your feet in preparation [to
face the enemy with the firm-footed stability,
the promptness, and the readiness produced
by the good news] of the Gospel of peace.*
—EPHESIANS 6:15, AMP

O UR HEARTS ARE encased in the righteousness
of God by the breastplate of righteousness,
and the fruit of righteousness is internal and
external peace.

And the effect of righteousness will be peace
[internal and external], and the result of righteousness will be quietness and confident trust forever.
—ISAIAH 32:17, AMP

At the birth of Jesus Christ, for the first time, peace and
goodwill to men on Earth was announced by the angels
from the heavenlies without man bringing a peace offering
to God (Luke 2:14)! The world uses the word *peace* as a

ceremonious language or formally as a greeting or during deliberations at meetings, but what the world calls peace is a fleeting sense of quiet or well-being. You can only give out to others what you possess. The world cannot give peace because it does not possess peace. The world does not know peace. Peace is not a thing, but a person and He is Jesus. Jesus is the Prince of Peace (Isa. 9:6).

Jesus is our peace with God, with the Jewish nation, with each other in the Body of Christ, and with ourselves, knowing that we have been forgiven our past trespasses (Eph. 2:14, 19). Jesus purchased our peace with God by His blood (Eph. 2:13). The chastisement of our peace was upon Him (Isa. 53:5).

> Peace I leave with you; *My [own] peace* I now give and bequeath to you. Not as the world gives do I give to you. Do not let your hearts be troubled, neither let them be afraid. [Stop allowing yourselves to be agitated and disturbed; and do not permit yourselves to be fearful and intimidated and cowardly and unsettled.]
>
> —JOHN 14:27, AMP
> (EMPHASIS MINE)

Jesus gives His disciples His peace. This is His legacy He bequeaths us with, and that is why the devil does everything he can to cause us to let go of it. Peace is our inheritance from Jesus. Therefore, do not allow your heart to be troubled or afraid. This is a choice you have to make.

> When a man's ways please the LORD, he maketh even his enemies to be at peace with him.
>
> —PROVERBS 16:7

It is not compromise with the enemy that brings peace to us, but walking right before God in all situations, which allows Him to release His ordained peace for us (Isa. 26:12); this peace manifests in every situation, even with our enemies! The kingdom of God is righteousness, peace, and joy in the Holy Spirit (Rom. 14:17). We go into battle in the fullness of the kingdom and declaring the kingdom of God. Let us consider the role of the gospel of peace in spiritual warfare.

> How beautiful upon the mountains are the feet of him who brings good tidings, who publishes peace, who brings good tidings of good, who publishes salvation, who says to Zion, Your God reigns!
> —Isaiah 52:7, AMP

This scripture was quoted again by Paul in Romans 10:15. The word *beautiful* in Hebrew is *na'ah* which means properly to be at home.[1] "Upon the mountains" means the presence of God. "Good tidings" means good news with cheerfulness. "Publishes peace" or "publishes salvation" means to perceive or understand by reason of attention and obedience to the Word so that you are able to publish or proclaim peace or salvation, i.e., you live it first and then tell it. Therefore, when you receive the Word of God, you do so with rapt attention refusing to be distracted and not wanting to miss out on anything. Also, you want to do all that you hear the Word say with a view to proclaiming it. When you are publishing peace, it means you are already a peacemaker and abide in the peace of God. "Peace" means welfare, which is health, prosperity, peace, and rest in God. A peacemaker is constantly being in God's presence, and this is the kind of relationship we should have with God.

Blessed are the peacemakers: for they shall be called
the children of God.

—MATTHEW 5:9

People receive more from what they see you do than
from what they hear you speak. When people see that
your lifestyle does not align with what you speak, then
you are viewed as a hypocrite, and what you speak will
not be received. A hypocrite shall not come before God
(Job 13:16). That is why some believers are uncomfortable
when God's presence is manifest.

We are to be people who bring along with us hope and
not doom and gloom. We do not want people to say when
we are coming their way, "Here he comes again. I think
I better go get something because he is coming to say
something negative that will depress me," or say, "Here he
comes to criticize somebody." When you speak peace and
live it, you can walk into a situation where the people are
in confusion and chaos and tell them, "God reigns. It does
not matter what the circumstances look like; the devil is
not winning. God is winning because He is in control."
We are bearers of hope in Jesus Christ. The word *hope*
indicates some expectation of obtaining the good desired
or the possibility of possessing it. Hope therefore always
gives pleasure or joy. Speak hope, salvation, victory, over-
coming, and conquering into situations.

Therefore, if we paraphrase Isaiah 52:7, it reads, "How
properly at home in the presence of God are the feet
of him who brings good news with cheerfulness, who
perceives or understands by reason of attention and
obedience to the Word so that he is able to publish or
proclaim peace, health, prosperity, and rest by living it
first and then telling it; who brings good news with the

cheerfulness of expected good, not of doom and gloom, but of hope; who says to the people of God, 'Your God and not the devil reigns.'"

When I was in the university in the 1970s, I always chose roommates who were members of the Scripture Union (SU). I never wanted to be roommates with an unbeliever like me, because I knew that the only way I could share a room with someone and have peace was to share it with a believer, even though I had refused to give my life to Christ. One of the excuses I gave for not giving my life to Christ was that most of the girls who were believers looked so morose and drab. They did not even remember to comb their hair, and some did not put on jewelry. I said that I did not want to look that drab because I thought that God was making them look like that. Believers should remember that they are ambassadors for Christ. You can look trendy and yet be Spirit filled, tongue talking, Word speaking, and sanctified in the Lord. When you are dressing up in the morning, remember that you are dressing up as an ambassador for Christ. Have you ever seen an ambassador looking drab? He always looks good so that when you see him, you have to ask, "Who is that?" Even when an ambassador has to hurriedly go out of his house, he puts on something decent because he is not representing himself, but his country. We belong to the kingdom of God, and we have a King whose name is Jesus. He has personally sent us as His ambassadors on planet Earth to reconcile people to God through Him. In Colossians 1:20, we are told that God has made peace with man through the blood of Jesus' cross and reconciled all things in heaven and Earth to Him.

Jesus said in John 14:27, "Peace I leave with you, my

peace I give unto you: not as the world giveth, give I unto you. Let not your heart be troubled, neither let it be afraid." Do not be afraid because Jesus has given you His peace. All you need to do is to receive it. You cannot use the world's standard to qualify Jesus' peace. In the midst of the storm at sea, Jesus was asleep on a pillow in the boat while His disciples were having a panic attack (Matt. 8:24–25). Jesus' peace served Him. On the way to the Cross when Jesus was brought before the Sanhedrin, the religious leaders reviled Him, but He never reviled them back (1 Pet. 2:23). This was a difficult time, but He kept His peace and did not allow anything in this world to touch it or take it away from Him. Peace is not necessarily the absence of turmoil, but it is the presence of someone—Jesus, and His release into a situation changes your options. Your peace is not dependent on what is happening with the elements around you, but on who lives in you. Jesus is the Prince of peace; God the Father is the God of peace; and they both have their abode in you.

The peace that Jesus gives you is not only to serve you but also to dissipate into your household and into those who come into the sphere of your life. Jesus has instructed us to release our peace into every worthy household we enter (Matt. 10:12–13). Jesus gives us His peace so that we can patiently stand constant and resolute on His Word in order to experience His promises. This is pervasive peace which means peace passing through the whole extent of a thing from beginning to end. That is why Jesus said that His peace that He gives you is not like that that the world gives you, which is temporary.

Ephesians 2:14 tells us that Jesus is our peace! If you have Jesus living in you, then you have the peace of God in you. When there are circumstances and chaos around you, the battle is not for your finances or health, etc., but for your soul. All these circumstances are distractions! The enemy wants to deface (mar) your soul and make you back down on the Word of God that you believe for your life. Do not give the devil room in your life. Do not let the devil tag or attach to you. If he tags you, he can always call up the tag in you, and then you become like a robot that he maneuvers because his spirit identifies with his tag in you! Do not let the devil have anything in you. Jesus said that the devil had nothing in Him (John 14:30). You too should be able to say, "The devil has nothing in me. The devil has nothing in my household. I will not allow the devil to tag me with bitterness, malice, or unforgiveness."

Let us discuss further the footwear of a Roman soldier's footwear, which was in two parts: the greaves and the caligae.

GREAVES

The greaves covered the Roman soldier's legs from his knees to the top of his feet. They were made of metal, beautifully crafted, and were specially shaped to wrap around the calves of a soldier's legs. They were custom fitted to the calves and bound tightly with leather strips. Our legs need to be tightly fitted with the Word of God and the peace of God. The only way we can have a custom fit with the peace of God is when we spend time in His Word and in His presence. We need to be people of the Word of God and prayer, accustomed to being in God's presence. The greaves were essential for protecting the soldier's legs when he was required to march through rocky and thorny terrain. It was not just where he placed his feet that mattered, but also that he should not scrape his shin or calves. If he did not have the greaves as protection for his legs, he would be gashed and cut by the environment. Some of us are bleeding from the injuries sustained from our environment because we have not put on the greaves that God has given us to protect our legs.

Thus, the greaves gave the soldier protection so he could keep walking, regardless of the obstacles he encountered. There is only one direction in which we are to move in God, and that is forward. Luke 9:62 says that the one who has put his hands to the plough and looks back is not fit for the kingdom. Hindrances and obstacles will come, but the Lord says, "Move forward!" The only way you can move forward is if you have the correct footwear. Have you ever attended a function and worn the wrong foot-wear? This especially applies to ladies. A lady puts on a beautiful pair of high-heeled shoes that are tight fitting or have a steep slant; after church service, she decides to go get some groceries. If the shoes are tight or uncomfort-able, she will start walking awkwardly and will not be able to finish buying what is on her grocery list even though she needs them. It will be pure torture walking the aisles of the store. She aborts her shopping, quickly leaves the store, and removes her shoes as soon as she gets into the car. The shoes of peace God gives enable us to finish the task at hand.

We need to remain faithful in the midst of adversity. Some of us give up too easily. We need to be steadfast in our undertakings, especially in things pertaining to God and His house. God is looking for a faithful generation that will not deny Him when they are in the midst of turmoil or adverse conditions. The Israelites did not and could not remain faithful when in the wilderness. They murmured many times, doubted God's Word, denied God on several occasions, and rebelled against the leader appointed over them by God. Can you remain faithful to God no matter the condition? God is looking for resilience in us. The resilience of a substance is its ability to spring back to the former shape or position when the pressure put on it is removed. For example, rubber is more resilient than wood. When pressure is applied on both, wood will break faster. Rubber will remain intact, though there might be some slight bending, but once the pressure is removed, it bounces back to its original shape and position. It can take the pressure and remain whole. That is how we should be! Adversity comes to everyone in different forms, but for the believer in right standing with God, God's favor pulls you through intact. Remaining faithful to God in times of adversity is what will pull you through, so do not give up. Adversity never stopped the disciples from preaching the gospel of Christ.

> Though I walk in the midst of trouble, thou wilt revive me: thou shalt stretch forth thine hand against the wrath of mine enemies, and thy right hand shall save me. The LORD will perfect that which concerneth me: thy mercy, O LORD, endureth for ever: forsake not the works of thine own hands.
>
> —PSALM 138:7–8

The greaves also gave the soldier protection in those moments when an adversary kicked him in the shins, trying to break his legs. The greaves prevented legs from being broken; thus, the enemy's attacks were in vain.

Situations try to break your stand in the Lord and His Word, but if you have your greaves on, when the enemy hits you, he hits the greaves. Instead of your legs breaking or your knees buckling over, the enemy is bruised and wounded and has to retreat.

No matter how skilled you are as a soldier or warrior in Christ, if your legs or feet are injured, you cannot stand to fight, and it is important to stand your ground in this fight. Ephesians 6 keeps on emphasizing the word *stand*. Before, during, and after the fight, you keep on standing. That is the posture that God created us to assume. It is only when you stand that you have a place to fight. Just as the greaves of a Roman soldier protected him from the environment and from the blows of his enemy, the peace of God, when it is operating in your life, protects and defends you from the hassles and assaults of the devil. The enemy may try to disrupt, distract, or steal your attention by causing negative events to whirl all around you. However, his attempts will fail because the peace of God, which is like these protective greaves, stops you from being hurt and enables you to keep marching forward impervious to the devil's attempt to take you down! The Lord wants you to come out of every situation whole because this serves as a testimony of His power, goodness, and mercy. Our peace with God produces peace in us which makes us to be at peace with others, no matter the circumstance.

> Great [*abundant*] peace have they which love thy law [*hear and obey the Word of God*]: and nothing shall offend [*be a stumbling block, obstacle, cause*

to fall due to hesitation arising from the difficulty of
determining what is right or expedient] them.

—PSALM 119:165

(EMPHASIS MINE)

Offence is a stumbling block which hinders your walk and allows the enemy to have a devastating effect on you in battle. When wearing the greaves, you keep on moving forward remembering the Word of God. When an individual at your workplace starts acting up, you remember that what you owe all men is love. When lies are told about you to your boss by your colleague, you remember that the Word of God says that you bless your enemy because this will be like coals of fire on his head.

Be careful for nothing; but in every thing by prayer and supplication with thanksgiving let your requests be made known unto God. And the peace of God, which passeth [*superior to; above*] all understanding [*all intellect*], shall keep [*mount guard as a sentinel; hem in, protect*] your hearts and minds through Christ Jesus.

—PHILIPPIANS 4:6–7

(EMPHASIS MINE)

A sentinel's duty is to guard the gate. He does not just stand in one place, but he marches around and peers to see whether an enemy is coming. A sentinel is armed so that he can deal with the enemy when he shows up. When you are wearing the footwear of peace, the peace of God, which is above all intellect, becomes a sentinel to your heart. When fear wants to come into your heart, the peace of God knocks it away. It does not allow fear to captivate your heart. When that unexpected devastating news comes and you are just about to say, "O God, why me?" the peace of God brings up a scripture to your heart, and you hear in your spirit, "You are not forsaken. The Lord will never leave you nor forsake you. Though you pass through the waters, God is with you. The rivers will not overflow you, and when you pass through the fire, it shall not kindle on you. The Lord gives up people for your redemption." The peace of God can never be disturbed, no matter the amount of chaos going on around. Sometimes when we are going through some situation, we try to derive peace by doing such exercises as going shopping for new clothes or going away on holiday, but when we come back home, the problem emerges again. It is only through Christ Jesus that you can have the peace of God!

> Don't fret or worry. Instead of worrying, pray. Let petitions and praises shape your worries into prayers, letting God know your concerns. Before you know it, a sense of God's wholeness, everything coming together for good, will come and settle you down. It's wonderful what happens when Christ displaces worry at the center of your life.
> —PHILIPPIANS 4:6–7, THE MESSAGE

The peace of God, who is Jesus, displaces worries and anxieties from the center of your life. So what are you to think about? What should your mind dwell on if it is not to dwell on your worries?

> Finally, brothers, whatever is true, whatever is noble, whatever is right, whatever is pure, whatever is

lovely, whatever is admirable—if anything is excellent or praiseworthy—think about such things.

—PHILIPPIANS 4:8, NIV

This seems a mouthful. How can you remember what to think about? You can remember by using the mnemonic PREPLANT.

P: pure
R: right
E: excellent
P: praiseworthy
L: lovely
A: admirable
N: noble
T: true

Let this be in your heart and mind so that it will be a sieve to whatever comes in. If whatever comes in does not fall in line with any of these, the peace of God that is sentinel and mounts guard over your heart and mind will knock it out. In this way, when you are in adverse situations, all you can feel in your heart and mind will be the peace of God. The peace of God will protect and make you free from the onslaught and torment of worry, anxiety, strife, confusion, fear, chaos, and stress in your relationships.

CALIGAE

The caligae were heavy-soled military sandals which were worn by all ranks in the Roman army up to and including the centurions. The sandals were constructed from leather and laced up the center of the foot and onto the top of the ankle. The leather was well oiled to prevent decay. We need the anointing in everything we do. That is what preserves us in our walk. The steps, goings, companionship, road, progress, route, and journey of a good man are ordered, set up, established, fixed, prepared, appointed, and rendered sure by God, and He delights in his way because He set it up (Ps. 37:23). The sole was made of several thick layers of leather. Additionally, iron hobnails or spikes were hammered into the sole.

The word *shod* in Ephesians 6:15 in Greek is *hupodeó* which is a compound of the Greek words *hupo* and *deó*. The word *hupo* means "under," and *deó* means "to bind; bind under."[2] It conveys the idea of binding something very tightly under one's feet. Therefore, this does not give the picture of loosely fitted shoes but of shoes that have been tied onto the feet extremely tightly. You have got to hold tightly onto the peace of God through Christ Jesus because everything happening around you wants to rob you of it! If you only give the peace of God a loose-fitting position in your life, it will not be long before the affairs of life knock it out of place and away from you.

The word *preparation* in Ephesians 6:15 in Greek is *hetoimasia*, and it presents the idea of readiness or preparation.[3] When used in connection with Roman soldiers, the word *hetoimasia* portrays men of war who had their shoes tied on very tightly to ensure a firm footing. Once the Roman soldiers had the assurance that their shoes were going to stay in place, they were ready to march out onto the battlefield and confront the enemy. You need to be battle ready at any time to confront the enemy. You cannot allow your shoes to be loose in the midst of battle; otherwise, you will lose your footing and the enemy will strike you down! When a man's shoelace is loose, he runs the risk of tripping over it and falling down. You cannot afford to bend down to be tying your shoes while fighting! There is a depth of spiritual fitness through the peace of God from the Word of God and prayer that positions you in a state of readiness to fight the good fight of faith and win. When the shoes of peace are tightly fit on you, your faith is undeterred because you are ready to traverse any terrain.

The more securely the caliga fits the whole foot, with no movement of the caliga when marching, the better, because there will be no bruising or blistering regardless of the number of miles you march. When you are one with the peace of God, the devil cannot knock it off your life. The openness of the caligae with space in between the leather straps allowed airing of the feet, preventing athlete's feet, so that the soldiers could wear them all day. They could march and stand in them for long periods without experiencing discomfort. We are to be transparent in our Christian walk. Jesus was naked on the cross. The only thing that covered Him was His blood. In your walk, the only thing that should cover you is the sinless blood of Christ. You are not to have any hidden sin or agenda. Any hidden area in your life is a dark area for the enemy to tag you. The enemy develops the films of sins in your life in a darkroom, and when you least want them to surface— *voila!* here they come, because the devil has no mercy. You need to be quick to confess your sins, repent of them, and ask for God's forgiveness and cleansing from all unrighteousness (1 John 1:9).

The hobnails or spikes on the bottom of the caligae were to hold the soldier "in place" when in battle. When his opponent tried to push him down or around, the spikes on the soles of his shoes helped keep him securely in his place, making the soldier virtually immovable. Likewise, the peace of God will hold you in place when the devil tries to push you around! For this purpose, the concentration of hobnails was at the toes and heel for maximum traction. When the peace of God is in place in your life, it makes you able to hold on to faith in God for what you believe and not be distracted by the circumstances around you. The peace of God keeps you steady and still standing in tumultuous times.

On the other hand, one good kick with these shoes would inflict maximum damage on the enemy. Just a few seconds of stomping on a fallen adversary would kill him. There is no need for you to ever stop moving forward just because the devil tries to block your path. If he gets in front of you, just stomp (strike or beat forcibly with the hobnailed soles of your shoes of peace) in the peace of God all along the way! There is a song that Kirk Franklin released some years ago called "Stomp." During that period, there were some things going on in my life, and when I went to work, this was the song I kept playing in my car for a long time. I kept on saying, "Stomp!" Stomp with your hobnailed caligae on the enemy. Instead of the enemy's imprint being on you, the imprint of the soles of your shoes of peace will be on him.

Habakkuk 3:19 says that the Lord makes your feet like hind's feet. He makes you sure-footed. It does not matter how craggy the place you are in is, you are able to balance because of your hobnailed caligae. The Lord causes you to come out walking upon the high places of the Earth that God has destined for you. You navigate the difficulties of life through the peace of God because hobnails are not for smooth territory, but for rough terrain. Every place the soles of your feet tread shall be yours. This is what God told Moses and Joshua in Deuteronomy 11:24 and Joshua 1:3. Every place upon which you properly stand by treading with the hobnailed caligae of peace, you possess. The only way you can be secure in a place and say, "I possess my possession," is by wearing the shoes of peace.

> Through thee will we push down our enemies: through thy name will we tread them under that rise up against us.
> —PSALM 44:5

> Thou shalt tread upon the lion and adder: the young lion and the dragon shalt thou trample under feet.
> —PSALM 91:13

Lion in Hebrew is *shachal* which means the roar of a lion.[4] The enemy comes as a roaring lion. You tread down the noise of the enemy by the peace of God. *Adder* in Hebrew is *pethen* which means the twists and contortions of the adder.[5] These are the lies and schemes the enemy devises against you. You are to tread them under by the footwear of peace that God has given to you. "Young lion" in Hebrew is *kephir,* which means a young lion as covered with a mane or a village as covered in by walls.[6] It is from the root word *kaphar* which means to cover.[7] The dragon is Satan himself. Whatever evil the devil presents to you covered or uncovered; you shall trample them under your feet.

Behold, I give unto you power to tread on serpents
and scorpions, and over all the power of the enemy:
and nothing shall by any means hurt you.

—LUKE 10:19

Serpents represent anything that has come against you
that is sly, cunning, or artfully malicious—the works of
Satan. It represents the spirit of deception; this was the
principality in Egypt as the image of the serpent was
on top of Pharaoh's crown of office. Scorpions represent
things that pierce you, inflict pain, and sting you. Jesus
gives us power to tread on all these and over all the power
of the enemy, no matter what that principality is called.
Nothing at all shall hurt you. Nothing shall be an offender
to you since you refuse to take offense because of the
greaves of peace.

Great peace have they who love Your law; nothing
shall offend them or make them stumble.

—PSALM 119:165, AMP

Keeping and doing the Word of God produces length of
days, long life, peace, and undisturbed composure (Prov.
3:1–2). I have noticed that on days when I do not meditate
on God's Word, I easily lose my peace. Peace is tied to
the Word of God. The Word of God, Jesus, is the Prince
of Peace.

The church of Christ is the army of God on planet Earth.
When we are all wearing our hobnailed caligae of peace,
as we move in prayer and in the experiential knowledge of
the Word of God, what the enemy hears is the noise of a
battle-ready army. The sound of hobnails treading on the
ground presents as a loud, intimidating noise causing fear

in the enemy's camp. That is why the devil hates peace amongst believers and causes strife in churches! Instead of the enemy inflicting pain and fear in us, we are to do precisely the same to him as we walk in one accord in peace. The hobnails also kept the soles of the caligae from wearing out too quickly regardless of the length of the march or how long the campaign lasted. When the Roman soldier was given the greaves and caligae, the caligae were given to him without hobnails. The Roman soldier had to buy the hobnails for his caligae as they were not supplied by the army. To remain or dwell in the peace of God by faith is a choice you have to make. What is your choice? The peace of God is what we desperately need because that is what brings us out whole from every conflict or trouble we encounter. No matter what turmoil the enemy causes, you are to walk in peace. We are peacemakers because we are children of the living God (Matt. 5:9). We have a covenant of peace with God through Jesus Christ; therefore, wherever we go; we are carriers and dissipaters of peace. This is commanded peace.

> And he arose, and rebuked the wind, and said unto the sea, Peace, be still. And the wind ceased, and there was a great calm. And he said unto them, Why are ye so fearful? how is it that ye have no faith? And they feared exceedingly, and said one to another, What manner of man is this, that even the wind and the sea obey him?
> —MARK 4:39–41

When Jesus said to the sea, "Peace, be still," He released Himself or His Spirit into the situation. He commanded a replacement of the situation with His peace, and so He spoke to the sea to be still or silent. When God's peace pervades a situation, the enemy has to be silent because God's peace is greater. The lesser gives way to the greater.

The peace God gives you is beyond human understanding. Everything in your situation dictates that you should not have peace, yet you have the peace of God with you. Our Lord is the Shepherd who leads us beside the still and peaceful waters. Can you imagine the scenery? It is when the waters are still that you can absorb your environment and see what God has placed for you in your path. He restores your soul. He knows how to comfort, encourage, and strengthen you in your weakest moments. If you are despondent or feeling hopeless, He reminds you of the promises He has for you. He ministers to your body, soul, and spirit for wholeness. Then He prepares a table before you in the presence—not the absence—of your enemies. He is not afraid of your enemies. The King Himself lays a royal table before you, and when it is fully laid, He calls you and says, "This is for you." The only thing the enemy can do is watch you eat to your satisfaction because he cannot touch anything on the Lord's table.

At this table, every need of yours in the present and in the future is met because your times are in God's hands and He knows what you need to fulfill your purpose as ordained by Him. God did not just call you out because He had nothing else to do. He called you out to have success, victory, and triumph because you are called by His name. At the table of the Lord, He anoints your head with oil, and the anointing He bestows on you from on high permeates every area of your life—your finances, children, job, and business, etc. This is an overflow anointing which causes your cup at the table to have no choice but to run over with abundance, peace, comfort, provision, and health from God. When you then get up from the table, the only thing you can declare is, "Only the goodness and mercy of God shall follow me all the days of my life." The goodness and mercy of God become your sentries all the days of your life, so when poverty or anything contrary to the Word of God tries to follow you, they tell it, "Keep off," and knock it off. They are the only two sentries that have been mandated by God to follow you all the days of your life. Your location on planet Earth does not matter; only goodness and mercy shall follow you. Therefore, you will dwell forever and not just visit in the house of the Lord because you know that God alone is your source. Whenever you come to the house of the Lord, you have no reason to have a morose look. Having a sulky look on your face shows that you do not know the God you serve. You need to be excited! An experiential knowledge of God will make you able to avail yourself of what He provides for you. Experience God today and every day of your life.

ENDNOTES

1. *Na'ah,* "beautiful," Strong's H4998.

2. *Hupodeó,* "shod," Strong's G5265.

3. *Hetoimasia,* "preparation," *Vine's Expository Dictionary,* vol. 3, 204.

4. *Shachal,* "lion," Strong's H7826.

5. *Pethen,* "adder," Strong's H6620.

6. *Kephir,* "young lion," Strong's H3715.

7. *Kaphar,* "to cover," Strong's H3722.

Chapter 5

SHIELD *of* FAITH

Above all, taking the shield of faith,
wherewith ye shall be able to quench
all the fiery darts of the wicked.
—EPHESIANS 6:16

YOU ARE TO take the shield of faith and superimpose or lift it up over the belt of truth, the breastplate of righteousness, and the shoes (greaves and caligae) of peace. Abiding in the knowledge of the truth, righteousness, and peace of God enables you to take and lift up the shield of faith. It is by faith you receive the truth of the Word of God. It is by faith you receive God's imputed righteousness (Rom. 3:22), and it is by faith you receive His peace! It is by faith that you stand (2 Cor. 1:24). You obtain a good report from God by faith (Heb. 11:2). Through faith, you have understanding that is beyond human logic (Heb. 11:3). You do all things in the kingdom of God by faith.

> Now faith is the substance of things hoped for, the
> evidence of things not seen.
> —HEBREWS 11:1

The first part of this scripture says "Now faith is" and
not "Now, faith is." So this is "Now faith." In 2 Kings
4:5, the widow moved *now* on the Word of God from the
prophet! In the now was the availability of the empty vessels. God is not limited by time, but what He does is in
time. Faith is for now! She followed the prophet's instructions exactly. Elisha instructed that when each vessel was
full, she should put it aside and pour oil into the next
empty vessel. Otherwise, she would have poured into the
empty vessels without necessarily filling each one to the
brim, thereby reducing the final quantity of oil in the
vessels and causing a shortfall in the total amount realized from the sale of the oil. We are to pay attention to
detail in God's Word to us. None of God's Word is to
be ignored or overlooked. The widow was asking for help
for her immediate need, but God was about providing for
her immediate and future needs. What God does is complete, but it is tied to our total obedience to His Word.
God's provision was as large as the widow was willing to
obey. God is able to do exceeding abundantly above all
that we ask or think, according to the power that works
in us (Eph. 3:20).

Faith is *the* (and not *a*) substance of things hoped for.
The enemy brings fear into your life so that you will forget
that you have faith. Faith gives you the ability to act over
your feelings. As long as you are conscious of your faith
in God and keep the shield of faith over your life, it does
not matter what is thrown at you; the shield of faith is
able to quench it. The shield of faith is not made of human

hands nor is it the shield of man; it is the shield of God, and nothing can penetrate it. The shield of God is big enough to cover you. God covers your head in the day of battle—you and your household—for He is a God of generations (Ps. 140:7)! Never lose hope, for your faith is hinged on your hope in God and His Word; He will never fail you. It is your hope in God that makes you to soar. It is your hope in God that makes you say, "Even though I do not see what I have asked God for today, I will yet see it." Never allow the enemy to steal your hope because when he does so, then he can steal your dreams and aspirations. To you it is hope, but to God it is the ingredient needed to give the substance called faith. Therefore, we need to encourage each other and always have an exhortation in our mouths (Heb. 3:13). Each time you exhort your brother, you are allowing his hope to soar, and when this happens, the enemy cannot lay claim on it.

Unfortunately, in contrary circumstances, we leave our hope lying on the ground where the enemy can trample all over it. Never lose your hold on hope; Jesus never did. For the joy that He saw before Him, He endured the Cross because hinged on hope is endurance. Hope tells you to keep on going on—that your time will come, and that you will not die but live and show forth the glory of God in the congregation of the living. Hope tells you that you can do it again—that you can get up from the ground, shake the dust off, and stand firm. Hope tells you that you can climb higher, and that there is a place to ascend, even as Caleb said, "I might be forty five years older, but I can take the mountains God promised me. I can take my possession" (see Josh. 14:10–12). When the enemy takes your hope, he steals the Word of faith from your mouth and therefore steals your destiny.

According to *Webster's Dictionary*, the word *hope* means a desire of some good, accompanied with at least a slight expectation of obtaining it or a belief that it is obtainable; confidence in a future event; the highest degree of well-founded expectation of good.[1] *Expectation*, according to *Webster's Dictionary*, is the act of looking forward to a future event with at least some reason to believe the event will happen.[2] Expectation is founded on prior information which renders the event probable. That is why we need to be constantly reading the Word of God with under-standing. The Hebrew word for "expectation" is *tiqvah*, which means literally a cord from God as an attachment to you. Are you expecting anything?

> My soul, wait only upon God and silently submit to Him; for my hope and expectation [*continually*] are from Him.
>
> —PSALM 62:5, AMP
> (EMPHASIS MINE)

The above scripture tells us who we are to expect from. Our expectation is not from man, but from God based on His Word—and He fulfills our expectation. When we base our expectation on man, we will constantly be disappointed. Base your expectation on God, and He will move whoever or whatever to get what you need done or provided for you! Our expectation is only in and from God! So since our expectation is from God, how do we wait on Him? Do we wait on Him musing and reckoning in our hearts that the possibility of Him coming through for us is fifty percent considering the circumstances? No!

We wait expectantly for Him with expectation in our hearts! How? Meditate on the Word of God—written, spoken, and impressed in your spirit, day and night like an animal chewing the curd till it is properly digested. Therein, you become one with the Word so that when situations put a squeeze on you, only the Word will come out of you. Expectation gives capacity and endurance to your faith. Hope in God and wait expectantly for Him, for you will yet surely praise Him—for He is your help and your God (Ps. 42:5).

> He only is [*continually*] my rock and my salvation [*deliverance, health, prosperity, help, rescuer of my destiny*]: he is [*continually*] my defence [*in Him, I am in an inaccessible place to the enemy*]; I shall not be moved [*waver, slip, shake, fall away from God's promise to me in His word for that particular situation or area of need*]. In [*not outside Him*] God is my salvation and my glory [*honor, splendor, copiousness*]: the rock of my strength, and my refuge [*shelter, place of hope*], is in [*not outside Him*] God. Trust in him [*be sure, confident*] at all times; ye people [*who?—us!*], pour out [*spill forth—when you spill something, the contents pour out uncontrollably*] your heart before him: God is [*continually*] a refuge for us [*who?—us, the righteous*]. Selah [*pause and think about this*].
> —Psalm 62:6–8
> (Emphasis mine)

I will thank You and confide in You forever, because You have done it [delivered me and kept me safe]. I will wait on, hope in and expect in Your name, for

it is good, in the presence of Your saints (Your kind
and pious ones).
—PSALM 52:9, AMP

You expect in His name because in His name all the
promises are fulfilled. When you wake up every morning,
what are you expecting from God for that day? You look
out for what you are expecting. Say what you expect! If
you are expecting a visitor to your home, you keep on
pulling the curtains aside to look through the window
because you are on the lookout for the one you are
expecting. Likewise, we should be on the lookout for what
God's Word says it will do, and all God's promises to us
are fulfilled in Christ Jesus!

An expectant mother knows without a shadow of doubt
that there is a baby in her womb which kicks within her
because the baby is alive. She also knows that the baby
in her womb belongs to her and that she will deliver the
baby. We are expectant with the Word of God, and the
Word will deliver what it says. The Word of God is like
rain and snow which come down to Earth from heaven
and do not return back, but water abundantly, slake the
thirst, satiate, and soak the Earth. They compel the Earth,
breaking through every barrier to bring forth as a midwife delivering a baby and bud or sprout fruit so that it
may give seed to the sower and bread to the eater. So shall
the Word that goes forth out of God's mouth be: it shall
not return to God as empty Word that cannot accomplish,
but shall accomplish, make, appoint, become, bring forth,
and yield that which God pleases. It shall push forward,
break out mightily, and be profitable and prosperous in
the thing to which God gave that Word (Isa. 55:10–11). The
Word of God is its own midwife to bring forth what it says.

Our expectation will not be cut off, aborted, or destroyed because it is in God (Prov. 23:18).

Hope furnishes the ground for expectation. This means that hope is not void. A Hebrew word for *hope* is *betach* which means to make refuge or a place of refuge.[3] Hope creates a place of refuge for you for that thing you are hoping for, protecting you from fear pertaining to that thing. Therefore, we have to remain in hope—a place of refuge.

What do you hope in that will never fail? The Word of God!

> They that fear thee will be glad when they see me;
> because I have hoped in thy word.
> —Psalm 119:74

Hope in God's Word because it is pure. It has been tried and tested and always comes to pass. The table of shewbread is called the pure table in Leviticus 24:6 and 2 Chronicles 13:11.

> Thy word is very pure: therefore thy servant loveth it.
> —Psalm 119:140

> Every word of God is pure: he is a shield unto them
> that put their trust in him.
> —Proverbs 30:5

> The words of the Lord are pure words: as silver
> tried in a furnace of earth, purified seven times.
> —Psalm 12:6

The number seven denotes completeness. The Word of God is completely pure. Nothing can be added to it or removed from it!

> Who against hope believed in hope, that he might become the father of many nations, according to that which was spoken, so shall thy seed be. And being not weak in faith, he considered not his own body now dead, when he was about an hundred years old, neither yet the deadness of Sara's womb: he staggered not at the promise of God through unbelief; but was strong in faith, giving glory to God.
> —ROMANS 4:18–20

Hope involves patiently waiting in expectation and not in fear. Abraham, our father in faith, did not allow the enemy to steal his hope, and so he was able to fulfill his destiny in God. Everything that Abraham's physical eyes could see did not give him hope, but he believed in hope that he might come into being what God had promised him—the father of many nations. As he held on to hope, his faith was not weak, but strong. Lack of hope weakens your faith. Abraham refused to dwell on the unfruitfulness of the two reproductive organs needed for procreation—his and his wife's. Instead, he had full confidence in God's Word. Abraham did not vacillate between belief and unbelief or doubt. He did not waver in believing God's Word but stood and walked in steadiness on the promised Word of God, and he gave glory to God before the manifestation of the promised Word.

Now the God of hope fill you with all joy and peace
in believing, that ye may abound in hope, through
the power of the Holy Ghost.

—ROMANS 15:13

Having all joy and peace about the thing that you
believe God for is the evidence that you are remaining
in hope. That is why you need to speak in tongues pertaining to the matter, so that you super-abound in hope,
and therefore your faith remains strong for that thing!

The word for *substance* in Greek is *hupostasis* which
means support, confidence, assurance, concrete essence, or
person.[4] The Amplified Bible refers to the word *substance*
as "title deed." A title deed entitles you to something spe-
cific (land, property, possession, etc.) and transfers it to
you either through purchase, inheritance, or as a gift. Our
lives have been purchased back (redeemed) from sin and
death to eternal life by the blood of Jesus (Col. 1:14). We
are heirs of God because we have been adopted through
Jesus Christ. Through Christ, we have been given power
to become the sons of God (John 1:12) and, therefore, joint
heirs with Christ (Rom. 8:17). All that God has belongs
to us through Jesus Christ. Without Christ, you are not
entitled to what God has, and salvation is the gift of God
(Eph. 2:8). The just (righteous) shall live by faith, which
means by faith they shall not die. Faith is what makes you
live, and this life is the God-kind of life, which is the way
Jesus lived when He was on Earth in the flesh. The only
way a believer must live the life that Jesus died to give us
is by faith. If we draw back from faith, God will have no
pleasure in us. When you draw back from faith, it leads
to perdition which is entire loss or ruin (Heb. 10:38–39).

Faith is reality! All things we see with our natural eyes

are shadows because they will fade away. Only what is birthed or borne by faith remains and endures because it is born of God. The real world of the believer is the world of faith. That is why without faith it is impossible to please God (Heb. 11:6). The world has corrupted the word *reality* to imply things we see and encounter in this realm. This has led to reality shows having top ratings now all over the world especially in the U.S. They focus people on the world and not on the Word of God for situations in their lives. The question that arises from these reality shows is, "How can I do life?" instead of "How can the Word of God give me wisdom to do life?" In reality TV, there is faith in everyone and everything else except in God and the Word of God. For example, in weight loss shows, the individual has faith only in his trainer to get him to attain the desired weight loss. You should exercise under a competent trainer, but have faith in God to give you the strength and discipline to get the job done. What is not born of faith is sin (Rom. 14:23).

> Then came the disciples to Jesus apart, and said, Why could not we cast him out? And Jesus said unto them, Because of your unbelief: for verily I say unto you, If ye have faith as a grain of mustard seed, ye shall say unto this mountain, Remove hence to yonder place; and it shall remove; and nothing shall be impossible unto you. Howbeit this kind goeth not out but by prayer and fasting.
>
> —MATTHEW 17:19–21

> And the Lord said, If ye had faith as a grain of mustard seed, ye might say unto this sycamine tree,

Be thou plucked up by the root, and be thou planted
in the sea; and it should obey you.

—LUKE 17:6

Jesus did not say, "If you have faith like the size of a
grain of mustard seed," but "If you have faith like or as a
grain of mustard seed." A mustard seed is the smallest of
seeds, but it has the capacity to become the biggest tree
of the herbs, and it spreads out its branches and birds
form their nests in them (Matt. 13:31). The mustard seed
does not question its ability to break through the soil to
become the greatest tree amongst the herbs. It just does
that which it was created to do. A mustard seed grows into
trees that occupy the particular piece of land where it was
sown by forming a thicket covering the ground in four to
five weeks and then growing to great heights. The mustard seed's taproots grow five feet into the ground. So the
mustard seed takes over below the ground, at ground level,
and at great heights above the ground. From one mustard
seed, you can get more than a hundred seeds.

Having faith as a grain of mustard seed means if you
have any faith at all, nothing will be impossible to you.
Faith authored by Jesus, the Word of God, is a taking-over
faith. It is faith that uproots and faith that plants. Talking
about your mountain is not what gives you the desired
result—but telling the mountain where it should go. Then
it moves to the place you sent it. You can speak to the
mountain to be removed to wherever you desire it to go,
never to come back, and it will obey you. A mountain is
anything that lifts itself above the knowledge and will of
God for you or a situation you are facing. A mountain is
anything that seems greater than you, looks insurmount-
able, appears permanent, does not go away, obstructs you

from going forward, or obstructs your vision. Prayer and fasting allow you to focus on God and His unlimited power, authority, and bountiful provision in all things.

On the other hand, the sycamine tree was a robust tree that grew to a height of thirty feet or more and was used for making caskets. It produced figs which were very bitter. The sycamine tree was known to have one of the deepest root structures of all trees in the Middle East; its roots went down so deep into the earth that it was very difficult to kill. Hot weather and blistering temperatures had little effect on this tree because it was tapped into a water source deep down under the earth. Cutting it to its base would not guarantee its death because its roots drew from underground sources of water, enabling it to keep resurfacing again and again. In other words, this tree was *very* difficult to eradicate. Yet, if you have faith as a grain of mustard seed, you can speak to the sycamine tree to be plucked from the root and planted in the sea, and it will do exactly as you have spoken. The sycamine tree represents bitter experiences that refuse to go away completely from us, but keep on coming back. The mountain and sycamine tree obey faith-filled words and not fear. Notice that faith is for *this* mountain or *this* sycamine tree. Faith is for what is before you or what you are dealing with now and not for tomorrow's potential problem.

> For whatsoever is born of God overcometh the world: and this is the victory that overcometh the world, even our faith. Who is he that overcometh the world, but he that believeth that Jesus is the Son of God?
> —1 JOHN 5:4–5

The word *overcome* in Greek is *nikaó* which means to subdue, conquer, overcome, prevail, or get the victory.[5] What is born of God overcomes the world; therefore, since faith is born of God (Jesus being the author and finisher of our faith), whatever is born of faith overcomes the world. The faith we are to have is the God faith, because faith does not originate from us, but from God's Word who is Jesus Christ in the flesh. Jesus is the author and finisher of our faith. An author is an originator or creator, and a finisher is someone who brings a particular task to completion. Jesus continues to create faith in your spirit until the day you will see Him face to face when you will no longer need faith to believe Him because you will see Him as He is. One is called an author when the work is complete and not while it is still in progress, e.g., a book or scientific paper for a journal. If your faith is as a grain of mustard seed, it is authored by the Lord; therefore, it is complete, enough to get the job done or overcome whatever situation is before you. When you author something, it is with a purpose in mind. Whatever faith Jesus authors in you, it is for God's purposes. Hebrews 5:9 tells us that Jesus is the author of salvation. He has completed the work of salvation, and there is nothing to be added to it.

Our faith is the victory that overcomes the world. The word *victory* in this sense is a noun, and it means conquest, a state of having won in war or in any struggle. The word *victorious* was not used, which is an adverb from the verb *victory* and means the act of winning. When we apply our faith to a situation, we are applying the already-established victory that overcomes the world. This means that our faith can overcome anything we come across in the world. That is why we are more than conquerors in Christ Jesus (Rom. 8:37). A conqueror is someone who has consistent conquests. He is unstoppable. In Christ, we are unstoppable by the enemy. God always causes us to triumph in Christ to make manifest God's knowledge in every place (2 Cor. 2:14). To conquer means to take control of a place or people by the use of military force. Our military force is our faith. The violent take the kingdom of heaven by force (Matt. 11:12), and their force is their faith. A conqueror is violent in conquest.

The second part of Hebrews 11:1 says that faith is *the* (and not *an*) evidence, proof, or conviction of things not seen. Faith is the only evidence or proof you need that God's Word will come to pass. The word *evidence* comes from the Latin word *evidentia* which also means proof and comes from the word *video* which means to see."[6] Faith, therefore, is that which elucidates or makes clear, enabling the mind to see truth. Without faith in God, you cannot see the truth manifest in the Word of God. When there is a situation, go to the Word of God and take time to settle yourself in it by faith till you have a divine perspective— because when things are in turmoil in your life, they unsettle you. A divine perspective means knowing what God will do according to His Word. Once this knowing by faith occurs, God will do it because He is not moved by wonder or doubt, but by faith. Having faith means that you are convinced that you have what you do not yet see with your physical sight. Faith invites you to experience the reality of truth.

For believers, faith is the eye of the spirit. Without faith, you cannot see spiritual things. A Spirit-led believer walks by faith and not by sight (2 Cor. 5:7). The word *walk* in

Greek is *peripateó*, which means to tread in all spheres of your life or to walk at large, especially as a proof of ability.[7] This infers that there had been resistance against you, but you have the breakthrough to walk in an enlarged place through faith. The faith walk is the proof of your ability as a believer and is to be exercised in every area of your life. As a believer, your path is the path of the impossible because it is faith in God that makes the impossible possible. That is why you are different. You might be asking the question, "Why am I always in hard places?" My answer to you is, "Do you know who you are? You are a believer with faith in God. Your faith in God makes the impossible become possible because God is the God of impossibilities. Why do you complain that you are different from others? Did you not know that you are different? That is why God calls you a peculiar treasure unto Him" (Exod. 19:5). Your faith walk does not acknowledge resistance. It is a walk of breakthrough, so it does not matter how tight the place the devil has cornered you into; your faith walk enlarges the place. God enlarges your steps so that you do not slip (2 Sam. 22:37). How does God enlarge your steps? By His steps which go before you as He has already gone ahead of you. His steps are larger than yours, and as you place your feet in His steps before you, your feet hold His steps (Job 23:11).

> Now the just shall live by faith: but if any man draw back [*from faith*], my soul shall have no pleasure in him.
> —HEBREWS 10:38
> (EMPHASIS MINE)

When we read a text, we see not only what is written, but also what is not written. The first part of Hebrews 10:38 says the just (righteous) shall live by faith. It therefore means that without faith, the just cannot live, but shall die. That is why you sometimes feel suffocated when you give way to doubt, despondency, and depression. Where is your faith? The new creation is designed to live by faith. Faith is your lifeline. When you speak in faith, you break the laws of nature. The Word of faith is in your mouth and heart (Rom. 10:8), hence you believe with your heart unto righteousness and confess with your mouth unto salvation (Rom. 10:10). You believe; therefore, you speak because you operate in the spirit of faith (2 Cor. 4:13).

> Elias was a man subject to like passions as we are, and he prayed earnestly that it might not rain: and it rained not on the earth by the space of three years and six months. And he prayed again, and the heaven gave rain, and the earth brought forth her fruit.
>
> —JAMES 5:17–18

The only way the born-again believer will be able to live the God-kind of life that is pleasing to God is by faith. God has designed us in Christ to live the God-kind of life which is *zoe.* Through continued faith in God, we are partakers of Christ (Heb. 3:14), and through Christ, we are partakers of the divine nature of God (2 Pet. 1:4). Without faith it is impossible to please God (Heb. 11:6).

He brought me forth also into a large place; he
delivered me, because he delighted in me [*only faith
pleases God*].

—PSALM 18:19
(EMPHASIS MINE)

Faith makes God bring you into a large place where
you have room to maneuver and be all that God has
called you to. It does not matter how many works you
have done or how much you have rendered in service
to God. The question is, "Whatever you have done, was
it done by faith?" For something to be done by faith, it
is normally beyond your ability. When tasks are being
distributed to individuals in the church, sometimes you
hear people say, "But I do not have the ability to do this."
That is why God is allowing you to be asked to do it so
that your dependence on Him will be 100 percent. It
will be obvious to you that there is no way you can get
the task done without the Lord. When the task is then
accomplished, it will be clear to you that it is 100 percent
God, and He alone gets the glory. If you want to please
God, your daily walk has to be a faith walk, and when
you walk in this manner, it is an exciting journey of life.
It is a constant journey of impossibilities becoming pos-
sibilities. When you walk the faith walk, it humbles you
because you know it is nothing about you; it is all about
God, and so you continually give Him the glory.

For example, suppose I am in need of a job and I keep
hearing that there is a particular man I must go through
before I can even be considered for the job. Apparently,
everyone that is presently working in the company had
to go through him. Then I start having faith in that
man to get the job I desire and look for who has a good

relationship with him to speak on my behalf. However, I want to hear what the Bible says about my situation and how my need can be met because Romans 10:17 tells me what I should be hearing to have faith in God—the Word of God. The Word is alive and speaks to my spirit, for the Word is Spirit and life.

I go to the Book of Philippians, chapter 4, and start reading from verse 14. Here, Paul is speaking to the Philippians, for they have been a giving church, giving not once, but on several occasions to meet his needs. Paul prays a prayer for them in verse 19: "But my God shall supply all your need according to his riches in glory by Christ Jesus." Paul is talking about a God in whom he has faith and about Jesus Christ in whose name he has raised the dead, healed the sick, cast out demons, been released from prison, delivered from perils, brought before kings, and had his needs met, etc. I know that I have been giving to the needs of the church, and so this Word applies to me. I take personal ownership of this Word, so I say, "But my God shall supply all my need according to His riches in glory by Christ Jesus." I keep on meditating on this Word which I have claimed as mine to get out of this situation of need, and I start thanking God for this Word He has sent to me. Remember, the Bible is the Word of God sent or given to us by God through the Holy Spirit inspiring holy men of God to write (2 Pet. 1:21). I know that this Word for me will not return void to God, but will accomplish that which He pleases and will prosper, flourish, and do well in what it says it will do (Isa. 55:11). Psalm 35:27 tells me that God takes pleasure in my prosperity.

I go to Proverbs 21:1 which says, "The king's heart is in the hand of the Lord; he directs it like a watercourse wherever he pleases." I lay claim to this Word and pray it for my situation. A watercourse is a natural or artificial passage through which water flows. Just as the direction in which water flows in a watercourse is governed by the design of the watercourse, the Lord directs the hearts of those in position of influence to give me the job according to His Word and purpose for my life. When I do come before this man for the job, my faith is in God doing what He has promised me in His Word and knowing that the Lord will use this man or any other person He decides to use to get me the job He desires me to have. When I look into the face of this man, my faith is not in his ability to do what I want, but in God's ability to give me my desire.

On their journey out of Egypt, the Israelites were caught between the Red Sea and the pursuing Egyptian army, but God told them to move forward instead of standing still. It was faith in God's Word and acting on it that caused the angel of God to change His position and move from being before them to behind them. By so doing, He came between them and their enemies, thereby protecting them and giving them light for safe passage. You move the hand of God by actions emanating from faith in His Word. Faith without works is dead (James 2:17).

The Roman soldier usually carried the *scutum*, which is a shield. This was a curved rectangular or oval shield which protected the soldier's front and sides and was to be used with other soldiers in the army to form a tortoise formation against the enemy. In the tortoise formation, the soldiers in front would hold their shields in front of them; those at the sides would hold their shields at their sides; and those in the middle would hold their shields above their heads. By so doing, they would move in one formation fully protected against the enemy. The scutum functioned best when the army was in tortoise formation.

However, this is not the shield mentioned by Paul in Ephesians 6:16 when describing the whole armor of God—because our God is a God of impossibilities. Has there ever been a time when you were in warfare and you could not readily get a sister, brother, or pastor to pray with you? Have you ever experienced a dark hour when you could not even mention to your best friend what you were going through? The Lord takes care of every situation because He does not want us to have 99 percent victory, but 100 percent victory. The shield Paul mentions is *thureos* which was inherited from the Greeks who probably got it from the Celts. Originally, *thureos* was the Greek word for door; it was a big stone used as a door for closing the mouth of a cave.[8] As the Greek language progressed, the same word was later used to describe their shield. The thureos was a large oblong shield which, unlike the scutum, was not curved, but door shaped. It was carried in the left hand and protected every inch of the soldier. The soldier did not need a fellow soldier in order to have every inch of his body to be protected. All he needed was his own thureos. You have to have faith in God for every area of your life because it is by your faith that you live. Let everything you do be done by faith in God because anything not done by faith is sin in God's sight (Rom. 14:23).

> Look at the proud; his soul is not straight or right within him, but the [rigidly] just and the [uncompromisingly] righteous man shall live by his faith and in his faithfulness.
> —HABAKKUK 2:4, AMP

Pride is equated with unrighteousness. Pride and faith cannot go hand in hand. The proud cannot have faith in God, although they might profess to do so, because they have faith in themselves and their abilities.

Faith is your confirmation. For example, when you are travelling to a particular city and you need to go by plane, you book your flight and have a confirmation, which assures you of a seat on the plane. When you get to the airport and they tell you the flight is full and there are no seats, you tell them you have a confirmation. It is the airline's business to get you to your destination, even if it means putting you in business or first class. Your responsibility is to get a confirmation. It is the same with hotel room booking. As long as you hold on to the room confirmation, you will get what is confirmed. Now, if you lose your confirmation, no one will listen to you.

You close every open door to the enemy in your life with your faith. You should not allow him entrance into your life. Whatever comes into your life has to come in through Jesus. If it is not through Jesus, you reject it. John 10:7, 9 tells us that Jesus is the door for the sheep. The word *door* in this scripture is *thura*, which is a root word.[9] When the Roman army would go out to battle using the thureos rather than the scutum, the enemy would say, "The people with the door have come." This is what the enemy should be saying about you because the door is Jesus. Jesus is the author and finisher of your faith (Heb. 12:2). When you lift up the shield of faith above all the armor of God, you are lifting up Jesus, who is the author and finisher of your faith as your banner.

The thureos was made of leather which was stretched over a wooden frame and decorated with the designs and emblem representing the soldier's service, century, and cohort. When the Roman soldier carried the thureos, you were not in doubt about where and who he belonged to because the emblem was on his shield. Who do you belong to? Do you display that you belong to Jesus wherever you go, even at your workplace? Wherever you go, you are supposed to carry the thureos. Behind the thureos was a hand grip which the soldier held, and in front was a rounded, metal protrusion called a "boss" that provided room for the soldier's hand to maneuver the shield in all directions. The faith of God can be used in every area of your life. The soldier also used the boss for deflecting blows from the enemy. This shield was used for personal combat by the soldier, so his protection did not depend on a formation, but on his shield.

Before the soldier went into battle, he drenched his leather shield with water so that the flames from the fire-tipped arrows of the enemy would be extinguished once they hit his shield. A dry shield would burn up and the soldier's protection would be lost. Is your shield drenched with the water of the Word of God, or are you going about carrying a dry shield so that the first fiery dart the devil throws at you causes your shield to burn?

Faith comes by hearing, and hearing (continual hearing) by the Word of God (Rom. 10:17). As you hear and receive the Word of God, faith is authored in your spirit by the Word of God who is Jesus. So, if you need faith for anything, go to the Word of God and read what it says about what you need. To hear the Word, you have to speak and continue speaking it; faith comes or is authored in your spirit for that need. The word of faith releases a walk of faith which releases works of faith. That is why you always need a "now" Word by reading the Bible on a daily basis. You do not read the Word of God only when you are in church. Some believers keep their Bibles tucked away all week and only bring it out when they are going to church. It is continual reading of the Word that will keep your shield of faith drenched with the Word of God. You cannot be living on the Word of yesteryears. I meet believers who are always talking about what God told them years ago. They never talk about what He is saying now. Is it that God has stopped speaking or that they do not have ears to hear the "now" Word since their ears have become so clogged up with what they are hearing in the world? What are you hearing? Are you constantly hearing God's Word on a daily basis? If so, do you believe God's Word that you hear? It is the Word of God you hear and believe that is the water that drenches your shield of faith and makes it function to protect you from the fiery darts of the devil. No fiery dart will remain unquenched. The Word of God cannot fail!

Fiery darts are fire-tipped darts or flaming missiles. Their purpose is to hurt or kill you by penetrating your shield or setting it ablaze. The fiery darts are thrown by the devil at all aspects of the armor. These flaming missiles are thrown at the breastplate of righteousness when the devil starts attacking you in your mind by telling you that you are probably not saved. He reminds you of your past sins and asks you how you can see yourself as righteous in such circumstances. You should remember that it is the imputed righteousness of God based on and produced by faith (Rom. 9:30). You did not work for it, but it was given to you by Jesus Christ. Therefore, you see yourself as righteous and say that you are the righteousness of

God in Christ Jesus. The fiery darts are thrown at your legs as the devil attacks your peace. You maneuver your shield of faith and cover yourself because God's Word says that He has ordained peace for you (Isa. 26:12). The devil will throw fiery darts at your belt of truth, making you doubt the Word of God. However, the Word of God says let every man be a liar and God be true (Rom. 3:4). Therefore, you have to keep on maneuvering your drenched shield of faith to quench all these fiery darts.

When the Israelites murmured against God in the wilderness, He allowed fiery serpents to bite them, causing heat, violent inflammation, and thirst, resulting in death for many of them. Those that survived did so by fixing their gaze on the brazen serpent on a pole that God told Moses to make and lift up above the congregation. This represented Jesus taking on Himself the sins of the whole world on the Cross. When the enemy attacks you during a trial, he causes intense heat in your life. Fixing your gaze on Jesus through continual meditation on the Word of God and prayer will make you continue holding up your shield of faith and cause your faith in God not to fail. Are you going through trials? Fix your gaze on Jesus because He has already given you victory.

In Daniel 3:21, Shadrach, Meshach, and Abednego were bound and cast into the fiery furnace which was made seven times hotter at the request of the king because they refused to bow down and worship the image erected by King Nebuchadnezzar. When they were being prepared to be thrown into the fiery furnace, one would have thought that they would first be stripped of their clothing. However, the opposite was done. They were fully dressed in their official regalia as leaders and then thrown into the furnace. The devil wants to humiliate the children of God and cause them to doubt God's promises. Being thrown into the burning fiery furnace with all their clothing on would make the flames leap more, increasing the heat and making the process of burning faster and more intense. Thank God the story did not end there. The Lord delivered these three Hebrew boys out of the fiery furnace, for He was with them in it. He took out the heat from the fire so that they were not burned, but came out without a hair singed or the smell of smoke on them. Faith makes you heat resistant.

It is the Lord that takes the heat out of your trials so you are able to go through. The only things that got burned in the fire were the ropes with which the enemy had bound the three Hebrew boys. As a result, they were loosed and seen walking about in the midst of the fire with the Lord. I bet they were walking about in the fiery furnace praising and worshipping God. Sometimes, your breakthrough while you are in the fiery furnace comes through praise and worship. Every piece of clothing signifying the status that God had given them did not change in color or get burnt in the fire. When you stay in faith, the devil has no power in the heat of trial to taint what God has given you. What God gives is without sorrow, and His gifts are without repentance (Rom. 11:29). As a result of this experience, King Nebuchadnezzar promulgated a decree stating that without a shadow of doubt, the God that the three Hebrew boys served was the true God. Stop complaining about whatever contrary situation you are in. Your breakthrough is on the way, and it will testify of the mighty God you serve. Without a test, there can be no testimony. You have to go through a mess to experience a miracle.

When Paul and Silas were bound in the stocks in the inner jail, at midnight when it was their darkest hour, they prayed and praised God as they faithfully fixed their gaze on the Lord. The result was a mighty earthquake that shook the foundations of the prison house where they were held bound. Their chains and the chains on all the prisoners were loosed, and all the prison doors opened! God is not only concerned about your deliverance, but also about all those who come into the sphere of your life.

What the enemy sends against us is fiery, so we need to hold up our shield of faith and make sure it is drenched in the water of the Word of God before the onslaught. The word *devil* in Greek is *diaballó* which is a combination of two words: *dia* which means channel of an act, means by, or through; and *balló*, which means throw after throw.[10] So, what the devil does is to come after you throwing fiery darts, one after the other to penetrate your shield or to get you weary from the constant onslaught so that you put down your shield. Only then can his fiery darts get at you and explode within you, releasing the spirit of fear so that you give up on God. The devil is not after your finances or job, etc. All he is after is your soul. As long as you are behind the shield of faith, you are protected from the fiery darts of the devil. So, hold it up above all the armor of God. It is not when the battle is raging that you want to start searching out the Word of God to drench your shield. Have you ever seen a soldier in the midst of battle going off to look for water? You have to be battle ready with your drenched shield. Once you sniff the enemy, up goes your drenched shield.

What enables you to keep on holding up your shield of faith when a battle becomes drawn out and weariness is about to set in? The answer is patience. According to *Webster's Dictionary, patience* means the suffering of afflictions, pain, toil, calamity, provocation, or other evil with a calm, unruffled temper; endurance without murmuring or fretfulness.[11] Romans 5:3 tells us that tribulation works out patience in us. The trying of our faith works out patience (James 1:3). It is like when you work out in a gym. The exercise, which is in no way pleasant, builds your muscles, making them firm and taut, and burns off the fat. So also is the trying of your faith; it builds up your "patience muscles" in the spirit and makes them firm. That is why you must allow patience do a perfect work in you to make you mature, complete, and wanting nothing (James 1:4). You have to have a passion of patience in Jesus Christ.

> I, John, with you all the way in the trial and the Kingdom and the passion of patience in Jesus, was on the island called Patmos because of God's Word, the witness of Jesus.
>
> —REVELATION 1:9, THE MESSAGE

In Revelation 2:2–3; 19, Jesus commends the churches at Ephesus and Thyatira for their patience. In Revelation, Jesus says this to the church in Philadelphia:

> Because you kept my Word in passionate patience, I'll keep you safe in the time of testing that will be

here soon, and all over the earth, every man, woman, and child put to the test.

—REVELATION 3:10, THE MESSAGE

Through faith and patience, you inherit the promises of God (Heb. 6:12).

But call to remembrance the former days, in which, after ye were illuminated, ye endured a great fight of afflictions [*pain, suffering, hardship*]; partly, whilst ye were made a gazingstock both by reproaches and afflictions; and partly, whilst ye became companions of them that were so used. For ye had compassion of me in my bonds, and took joyfully the spoiling of your goods, knowing in yourselves that ye have in heaven a better and an enduring substance. Cast not away therefore your confidence, which hath great recompence of reward. For ye have need of patience, that, after ye have done the will of God, ye might receive the promise [*after you have done the will of God, you will suffer affliction, but you must endure patiently with patient expectation while exercising your faith so that you can receive the promise. Without patience, you will not be able to hold on to faith and you will let it go*]. For yet a little while, and he that shall come will come, and will not tarry.

—HEBREWS 10:32–37
(EMPHASIS MINE)

We are appointed unto afflictions (1 Thess. 3:3–4), but not defeat. Therefore, do not allow what you are going through to move you from your confession of faith in Christ and the Word of God. When you hold up your shield, you are holding up your victory because it is your faith that overcomes and conquers everything in this world (1 John 5:4).

> I am crucified with Christ: nevertheless I live; yet not I, but Christ liveth in me: and the life which I now live in the flesh I live by the faith of the Son of God, who loved me, and gave himself for me.
> —GALATIANS 2:20

You live by the faith of Jesus Christ because He is the author and finisher of your faith. Your faith starts by and is accomplished by Jesus. How do you operate in the faith of Jesus who lives in you? By having the mind of Christ. This means having the thoughts, will, and emotions of Christ. How do you have the mind of Christ? Through the daily renewal of your mind by the Word of God and daily submission to the Word of God. By so doing, you are allowing Jesus to live in and through you. Jesus' faith never wanes. His faith is solidly in God the Father. We have boldness and access to God with confidence by the faith of Christ Jesus.

Genesis 2:2–3 tells us that on the seventh day God ended His work which He had made and rested from all His work. God blessed and sanctified the seventh day because that was the day in which He rested from all the work which He had made. The word *rested* in Hebrew is *shabath* from which the word *Sabbath* is derived.[12] God rested on the seventh day not out of fatigue, but because His work of creation was ended, finished, completed.

God created man on the sixth day, and on the seventh day, man entered God's day of rest. It was in this place of rest that Adam was to tend and keep the garden. Adam lived in the seventh-day rest of God. Man sinned by not believing God's Word; they chose to believe Satan (serpent) and were driven out of God's place of rest for them. To have stayed in God's rest depended on their continued belief of God's Word and living on the believed Word, which amounts to faith with works. We have to labor to enter God's rest and be careful not to come short of it through unbelief (Heb. 4:11, 1). The word *labor* in Greek is *spoudazó* which means to use speed, be prompt to, or be diligent to.[13] It gives the sense of quickly and carefully believing God's Word at all times! In Matthew 11:28, Jesus tells all who labor physically and are wearied and overburdened with anxiety and care to come to Him—and He will give them rest.

> And to whom sware he that they should not enter
> into his rest, but to them that believed not? So we
> see that they could not enter in because of unbelief.
> —HEBREWS 3:18–19

Belief in God's Word, which is faith, gives you entry into God's rest. Today, our rest is in Jesus and through Him, in God. Jesus is our seventh-day rest. On the Cross, Jesus said, "It is finished" (John 19:30). The work of redemption of man from sin and its consequences and reconciliation of man back to God is finished, complete, and made an end to. Rest in what Jesus has done for you. Whatever you do—whether it is prayer, believing God for something, or serving—you do all from this place of rest.

How do you remain in God's rest?

1. Fix your eyes on Jesus, the author and finisher of your faith, by fixing your eyes on

His Word. Your faith does not begin in you. It begins and is completed in Jesus. When Peter's eyes were fixed on Jesus, he could walk on the impossible (Matt. 14:29). God told Noah to put the only window in the three-storey ark in the roof and not on the side (Gen. 6:16). In so doing, the only way Noah could look outside was upward, and what he saw was the sky and not the devastation of the flood—dead bodies and animals— death all around. His eyes had to be focused on God throughout his time in the ark.

My heart is fixed, O God, my heart is fixed: I will sing and give praise.
—Psalm 57:7

He shall not be afraid of evil tidings: his heart is fixed, trusting in the Lord.
—Psalm 112:7

2. Keep out the spirit of fear. Do not let it get into you. This is a choice. People do crazy things due to fear of circumstances.

3. Refuse to focus or dwell on the circumstance around you. Do not allow yourself to be consumed by the situation.

4. Refuse the negative thoughts and scenarios that the devil will want to plague your mind with: What if this happened? What if the outcome is contrary? Did God really say? All this is so that you can doubt God's Word.

Doubt will take you away from God's Word, and when this happens, automatically you are outside Him. You stay in God by abiding in His Word. Jesus Christ is the Word of God. What the devil does is to take you away from what God has said. That is what he did with Eve (Gen. 3:1).

5. Let your mind be impregnated with the promises of God in His Word. Give no room to the devil in your mind. Bring every thought into captivity to the obedience of Christ—every thought submitted to the Word of God! This will lead to you speaking only the Word for that situation.

6. Fortify or strengthen your spirit by speaking in tongues. When your spirit is strengthened, it is no longer a struggle to refuse things of the flesh because your spirit is built up and stronger than your flesh. Now, you operate in the might of the Lord, for the Holy Spirit is the might of God.

But you, beloved, build yourselves up [founded] on your most holy faith [make progress, rise like an edifice higher and higher], praying in the Holy Spirit.

—JUDE 20, AMP

7. Feed voraciously on the Word of God, because the Holy Spirit uses the Word of God in you. The Word of God in you is the sword of the Spirit. At creation, the Holy Spirit hovered

upon the deep until the Word of God came. Then, He went into action. The Holy Spirit needs God's Word to do God's will.

ENDNOTES

1. *Webster's American Dictionary of the English Language*, s.v., "hope," (1828).

2. *Webster's American Dictionary of the English Language*, s.v., "expectation," (1828).

3. *Betach*, "hope," Strong's H983.

4. *Hupostasis*, "substance," Strong's G5287.

5. *Nikaó*, "overcome," Strong's G3528.

6. *Evidentia*, *Webster's American Dictionary of the English Language*, s.v., "Evidence."

7. *Peripateó*, "walk," Strong's G4043.

8. *Thureos*, "door," Strong's 2375.

9. *Thura*, "door," Strong's 2374.

10. *Diaballó*, "devil," Strong's G1225.

11. *Webster's American Dictionary of the English Language*, s.v., "patience."

12. *Shabath*, "rested," *Vine's Dictionary*, vol. 3, 311.

13. *Spoudazó*, "labor," Strong's G4704.

Chapter 6

HELMET *of* SALVATION

And take the helmet of salvation, and the
sword of the Spirit, which is the word of God.
—EPHESIANS 6:17

YOUR MIND IS a battlefield. This is where the enemy attacks most ferociously and where the war rages. It becomes essential, therefore, that you don protective headgear to safeguard your mind. The Lord has given us His helmet of salvation. The word *helmet* in Greek is *perikephalaia.*[1] It is a compound of the Greek words *peri* and *kephalē.* The word *peri* means "around," and the word *kephalē* means "head."[2] When you compound these two words, you discover that the word *perikephalaia* denotes a piece of armor that fits very tightly around the head.

> O GOD the Lord, the strength of my salvation, thou hast covered [*entwined as a screen; fenced in*] my head in the day of battle.
> —PSALM 140:7
> (EMPHASIS MINE)

There is a day (or days) of battle in an individual's life. This is what Ephesians 6:13 describes as the evil day. It is then that God who is the strength of your salvation entwines His salvation as a screen around your head, so that the enemy cannot take your head off. The Roman soldier's helmet was a fascinating and flamboyant piece of armor, very ornate, intricate, and highly decorated with all kinds of engravings and etchings. The helmet looked more like a beautiful piece of artwork than a simple piece of metal formed to fit snugly around the head of a soldier. We are not surprised at this because Psalm 149:4 tells us that the Lord beautifies the meek with His salvation. The Lord beautifies you with His deliverance. If not for the Lord's salvation, some of us would have been in the jailhouse, sick in the hospital, homeless, or in the psychiatric home, etc. The wages of sin is death, but the gift of God is eternal life through Jesus Christ our Lord (Rom. 6:23).

Salvation is a gift from God. That is why the helmet is so beautifully and skillfully done. Some of us have taken our salvation for granted. Always remember that it is a gift from God and not as a result of your works. There is no kind of work done by us that would have earned us salvation. It was not that we were so good; God did not look down on us and say, "Because they have been good and their report cards show many stars, My Son, go down and redeem them." No, we were all in our mess. Jesus did it alone for us, while we were yet sinners. What an awesome Savior! Your salvation is more precious that any gem on Earth. Your salvation is that which money can never buy. Your socio-economic or educational status or nationality can never give you salvation. This should always humble you and make you ever grateful to God. There are some of your peers that died at an early age and never received Jesus Christ as their Savior. Thank God for His grace, mercy, and forbearance toward you that He preserved your life.

Thank God you are called, chosen, and the elect of God. You are saved, redeemed, born again, and a new creation. When you wake up in the morning, you need to be excited. It is sad that people do not appreciate what they get for free. Salvation is a free gift of God, wrought in the precious blood of Jesus Christ.

The helmet was made of brass and was equipped with parts that were specifically designed to protect the head, cheeks, jaw, ears, and neck. It was extremely heavy; therefore, the interior of the helmet was lined with sponge in order to soften its weight on the soldier's head. This piece of armor was so strong—so massive and so heavy—that nothing could pierce through it, not even a hammer or a battle-axe. That is the salvation we have. We are fenced in and covered by God's salvation. That is why, even when you found yourself in certain situations, you went through them and are still standing. Others that encountered similar situations were taken down. The salvation of God is not just receiving Christ and being born again; it is a total package of deliverance from sin and its consequences: guilt, shame, sickness, poverty, low self-esteem, curses, etc.

You need to put your salvation tightly on your head, like a helmet. Sometimes, you might put it loosely on your head—and that is why on some days you feel saved and on others you do not. Hence, your knowledge of your salvation is dependent on how good the day is; this is subjective knowledge rather than objective knowledge of salvation. If your salvation is put on tightly, regardless of the circumstance, you will know that you are saved and that God loves you. It is His infinite love for us that caused Him to send His Son to die on the cross for our sins. I hear people sometimes say, "If I get this job, then I will know that God loves me," or "If I get my prayers answered, then I will know that God loves me." Such people do not know the God that they serve. God's love toward us is everlasting. He is an eternal God, and whatever He does is eternal. It is only what man does that is temporary.

The mind is located in the head as the middle ground between both ears. When you put the helmet of salvation tightly on your head, it protects your mind from the devil's onslaught of doubt and unbelief. Doubt and unbelief are seen as evil in the sight of God. Therein, you are saying God's Word is not true and call God a liar. This is what Satan did with Eve. He started by questioning and twisting what God had told Adam and substituted it with his own doctrine, which is directly contrary to the Word of God. Doubt leads to one having a double mind. James 1:6–8 says that he who doubts is like a wave of the sea, blown and tossed by the wind—rising high one moment and sinking another moment, believing one moment and not believing another moment. That man will not receive anything from the Lord. A double-minded man is unstable in all his ways. He wavers between what is right and what is wrong, between what is truth and what is a lie. Eve doubted God's Word, which caused her to become double minded. She chose to believe Satan's lie and ended up being deceived. Her deceived mind made her act out the lie she believed (2 Cor. 11:3).

When you expose your unprotected mind to the devil's insinuations, you place yourself in a position to be deceived. If you wear your salvation tightly over your mind, like the Roman helmet, the devil will not be able to deceive you about your healing, deliverance, prosperity, joy, well-being, or anything Jesus wrought for you on the Cross. As a child of God, you need to walk in the full knowledge of your salvation; otherwise, you will lose your head in the heat of battle. Salvation is not only what happens when you go to the altar to receive Jesus Christ as Savior. That is just the beginning. There is much more to salvation than that; it is a process.

> So do not worry or be anxious about tomorrow, for tomorrow will have worries and anxieties of its own. Sufficient for each day is its own trouble.
> —MATTHEW 6:34, AMP

Each day has enough of its own troubles. Do not worry about tomorrow's troubles. Plan for tomorrow, but do not worry or be anxious about it. If you do, it means you do not trust God to provide for your tomorrow. Planning for tomorrow as long as it is according to the Lord's guidance is time well spent, but worrying about tomorrow is time wasted. If we are not to worry or be anxious about anything, then what should we do?

> Be careful for nothing [*do not worry or be anxious about anything*]; but in everything by prayer and supplication with thanksgiving let your requests be made known unto God [*method of not being worried or anxious about anything*]. And [*when you do this*] the peace of God, which passeth [*is above, superior to, transcends*] all understanding [*intellect*], shall keep [*mount guard, garrison*] your hearts [*from*

which come the issues of life] and minds [*which is the battle field of the devil*] through Christ Jesus.

—PHILIPPIANS 4:6–7

(EMPHASIS MINE)

You might say, "I pray and give supplications with thanksgiving, yet I still find myself worrying about the situation that I have prayed for." That is because you did not pray a prayer of faith. Worry comes as a result of fear about the situation and its outcome. The root of worry is fear. Worry is borrowing trouble and acquiring burdens from tomorrow. It leads to illnesses, e.g., hypertension, diabetes, or death from heart attack or stroke. Worry brings about confusion and fatigue. People that worry get easily tired. The cares of this world—worry and anxiety—choke out the Word of God in us, and therefore choke out our faith and make us unfruitful.

Roll [*roll away from you*] your works upon the Lord [commit and trust them wholly to Him; He will cause your thoughts to become agreeable to His will, and] so shall your plans be established and succeed.

—PROVERBS 16:3, AMP

(EMPHASIS MINE)

We need faith to live every single day if we are to reap, partake, enjoy, and live in all the promises God has given us through Christ Jesus. These promises enable us partake of the divine nature of God. That is the kind of life the new creation in Christ is meant to live—life to its fullness in Christ; our sufficiency is of God (2 Cor. 3:5). The word *sufficiency* means a supply which is enough, meaning as much as is needed for a purpose, indicating no lack.

Therefore, sufficiency and purpose are linked together. The word *enough* usually comes before a plural or uncountable noun, e.g., enough houses, cars, or shops (which are plural nouns)—or enough food or money (which are uncountable nouns).

> And her merchandise and her hire shall be holiness to the LORD: it shall not be treasured nor laid up; for her merchandise shall be for them that dwell before the LORD, to eat sufficiently, and for durable clothing.
>
> —ISAIAH 23:18

Sufficiency in God is relying on His ability to bring things to pass in your life just as He said He would do. God knows all that you need (Matt. 6:32). Your need does not take Him by surprise! Do not lose your focus from God. Do not forget the kingdom to which you belong. It is a kingdom in which there is full provision for its citizens. Sufficiency in God is dependent on your faith level because His Word is true and has remained the same through the ages past. What can you believe God for? Do you believe His Word is true? His Word will come through for anyone who believes and acts on it. Ask the Lord. Open your mouth wide, and He will fill it for you (Ps. 81:10). Ask in faith, nothing wavering. He is the God who makes all grace (all of God's ability) super-abound toward those who believe in Him, that that they will always have all sufficiency in all things so that they may super-abound to every good work (2 Cor. 9:8)!

> For though we walk in the flesh, we do not war after the flesh: (For the weapons of our warfare are

not carnal, but mighty through God to the pulling down of strong holds;) casting down imaginations, and every high thing that exalteth itself against the knowledge of God, and bringing into captivity every thought to the obedience [*submission, attentive hearkening*] of Christ.

—2 Corinthians 10:3–5

(Emphasis mine)

The things mentioned in the above scripture all have to do with the mind. Imaginations are in the mind. Anything contrary to the Word of God that you esteem higher than the Word of God becomes exalted against the knowledge of God in your mind. This is the lie of the devil. You must bring every single thought into captivity to the obedience of Jesus Christ. This is not a passive action but an active one. God has given you the enablement and power, through Christ, to do this. We all struggle with our thought life because the devil tries to penetrate our minds with thoughts that are contrary to the Word of God. However, it is your duty as a believer to have a guard over your mind, and you have the Word of God to do so. Some believers behave as if they are paralyzed and allow thoughts contrary to the Word of God to come streaming into their minds. All they say is, "What do I do? This thought just came." You have authority over your thoughts through the Word of God. That is why you need to know the Word of God—because whatever the devil throws at you, there is a word for it. Whatever the devil threw at Jesus, He had a word for it. He kept on saying what was written in the Word of God, and the devil left Him for a season. Then the angels of God came and ministered to Him (Luke 4:13).

Your sufficiency is in the Word of God. You cannot just

allow any thought to go through your mind. You are not a trash can. How would you feel if each time your neighbor had trash, he knocked on your front door, and when you opened it, he threw the trash into your living room? I do not think you would be too sanctified to keep quiet! However, this is what we do with our minds. We allow the enemy to stroll into the sphere of our minds and dump his trash—leaving our minds cluttered, confused, and in a constant state of chaos. It comes to a point where we lose clarity about the Word of God. We keep on asking ourselves, "Did God say this?" Do not allow the devil access into your mind! Not even for a few seconds. Your mind is holy ground for God. You were formed in His image and after His likeness. That is why the Bible says that the born-again believer has the mind of Christ (1 Cor. 2:16).

It is your duty to guard what comes into your mind. You have power and authority to do so. Actions first start with thoughts. If you dwell long enough on your thoughts, they will bear fruit. How do you know that it is the enemy bringing a thought to your mind? When that thought is contrary to the Word of God. When you are in the super-market and have a thought to steal an item from the shelf, that thought is not from the Holy Spirit but from the devil. When you come in late to work and you have the thought to sign that you came in early, that thought is not from the Holy Spirit but from the devil. After falsely signing in early, then you say, "Hallelujah, I was not caught today." When the devil brings contrary thoughts to us, our plumb line is the Word of God. When the devil brings to you a thought contrary to the Word of God, do not take it! Do not receive it. You speak out, "I do not take this thought. I refuse it."

A thought cannot gain entry into your mind without

your permission. If you are flooded by contrary thoughts or thoughts of suicide, it is because you permitted it. Contrary thoughts usually start with self-pity: "See, how I have been treated." When you dwell long enough on these contrary thoughts, you feel that the whole world is against you. Before you know it, you feel like jumping out of the window. It does not matter what people are saying about you; for those thoughts to get into you, you have to permit their entry into your mind. Nobody can force a thought on you. Teenagers usually give the excuse of peer pressure. Unfortunately, there are some adults who behave like teen-agers. You should counter contrary thoughts by speaking the Word of God relevant to that situation.

It is not enough just to think about not accepting the thought, but you must speak out the Word of God to counter the thought. The spoken word is higher than a thought. That is what Jesus did when he was tempted by the devil, right after He came out of the wilderness having fasted for forty days and nights. You can either take all your thoughts captive, or your thoughts will take you captive and bring you to a place you really do not want to go. The devil will floor you in the area of reasoning and reckoning because he has been around for a much longer time than you. He is the old serpent (Rev. 12:9; 20:2). He is described in Ezekiel 28:12, 17 as being full of wisdom, but the scripture also says that he corrupted his wisdom because of pride! That is why he is cunning and sly. However, there is something you have that he does not have: faith. So, you should always stay in the arena of faith in the Word of God—it is a no-go area for him. Do not stay in the arena of human reasoning and reckoning! Satan can quote scriptures, but he has no faith in the Word of God or in God.

We must spend time studying what the Bible has to say about God's promises to us—about our healing, deliverance, His desire to bless and prosper us, the promises of God for our seed, and the benefits of our redemption in our everyday lives. It is not your cell or life group leader who will study the Bible for you. Studying the Word of God takes time and sacrifice. There is no shortcut or microwave formula for this. You have to go the long haul and study the Word of God for yourself. You are to live every day of your life redeemed. You do not live six days of the week like a devil, and then on Sunday you go to church. Your salvation is not like a light switch that you turn on and off, depending on the environment that you find yourself in. You live your life redeemed at home, at work, in the supermarket, in the bank, and wherever you go.

Your comprehension of all that salvation encompasses must be ingrained in your mind. When your mind is convinced of these realities and is trained and taught to think correctly in terms of your salvation, then the revelation knowledge of salvation becomes a helmet for you! It is only then that you can operate with a sound mind (2 Tim. 1:7). It is only with the mind of Christ that you can understand what Christ has done for you. It will not matter how hard the devil tries to hack away at your mind; you know beyond a shadow of doubt what Jesus' death and resurrection purchased for you. When your thoughts are covenant conscious, your life will manifest the covenant promises! When we were in the world, we lived like the devil, and there were certain "lingoes" which, when spoken, we immediately knew what they meant. That was a different way of life. God has brought us out from darkness into His kingdom. Now that we are in the kingdom of God, we have to learn to speak kingdom. The first language that you usually teach your child before he starts attending school is your native language. When the child starts attending school, he has to learn English or the language of communication in the school. It would be very worrying if the child continued speaking his native tongue in the class. That would not be allowed. Some believers are still speaking their native tongue—the lingoes they learned in the world when they were in the kingdom of darkness—and they are trying to apply it in the things of God. It will not and cannot work because in the kingdom of God, there is a different language—the Word of God. You cannot obey the laws of one kingdom and get the benefits of another. That is why God says that the Word of God should never depart from our mouths, but we should meditate on it day and night so that we are careful to do all it says (Josh. 1:8).

As children of the kingdom of God, we need to train and teach our minds to think salvation. Then, our thoughts will no longer be contrary but the same as the Word of God. God told the Israelites to speak the Word of God, to teach their children His Word and His ways when they were sitting, standing, or lying down as long as there was breath in them (Deut. 6:7). When you do this, speaking the Word of God becomes a way of life. This cannot happen when you do not read your Bible during the week except when you come to church. Then, when you see your brother in the church, you say, "Praise the Lord, brother. I have been battling with the devil all week." You have to train your mind to have sanctified thoughts. If your mind is so trained, then when the devil throws a thought at you, instead of dwelling on it, the Word of God in your mind immediately ejects it and says, "Not allowed here."

We have the mind of Christ. This means training your mind to think the Word of God. This is a process that comes not through mere acquaintance, but through intimacy with the Word of God. So, when the devil throws a thought at you saying, "Everyone in your lineage has been poor, so no matter how hard you work, you will remain poor," you will know that this is contrary to the Word of God. You will say, "I will not take this thought because the Word of God says He gives me power to get wealth." When your mind is trained to think the Word of God, it responds instantly with the Word of God. You do not have to book an appointment to see the pastor or go to a deliverance team to pray deliverance over you from contrary thoughts. Instead, your mind dwells on the promises of God for you in His Word. In your mind, the Word of God is the answer and the solution. No matter how despondent you are, because your mind is trained with the Word of God, the Word of God rises up to counteract anything that comes against you. When your boss is trying to intimidate and humiliate you, your mind says, "The Bible says, 'I am the head and not the tail.'" When people say you are not beautiful, do not have a good figure, or are too short, your mind tells you, "I am wonderfully and fearfully made." Our minds need to think the Word of God.

Our covenant is a perpetual agreement between us and God through Jesus Christ. God never changes. He never breaks His covenant, so the onus is on you to do likewise. If you know that you are serving a covenant-keeping God, and the promises He has given you in His Word are by covenant in the blood of Jesus Christ, then your mind should be able to receive whatever the Word of God says. This is a better covenant built on better promises that are eternal. Therefore, when sickness comes your way, your mind should say, "I have a covenant of healing through Christ Jesus. The Lord has told me that when I walk upright in obedience to His word, the diseases He put upon the Egyptians shall not come on me. So sickness (call it by name), get out of my life." You have the authority to forbid what is contrary to the Word of God coming into your life and into your household. When the Israelites were coming out of bondage in Egypt, God told them to put the blood of the lamb that they had as a covenant with Him on the doorposts and lintels of their houses. So, when He saw that, He would tell the destroyer to pass by because "I have a covenant with this one." The blood of Jesus is upon your life, so when the enemy comes raging and throws the kitchen sink at you, you should say, "The blood, the blood. Torment, you cannot come in here. I forbid you."

A husband and wife who have intimacy and an understanding of each other do not need to verbalize this in public. While you are seated next to them, they can be having a non-verbal conversation because they know each other's mind. We have the mind of Christ, so we should know what is on Christ's mind and not have any thought that Christ does not have. The mind of Christ has no evil thought, no depression, no unforgiveness, and no defeat. It is Christ's mind that gives us sound minds. As a believer, you cannot afford to have a sick mind filled with what is contrary to the Word of God. The devil is called Beelzebub which means lord of the flies. Flies are attracted to death and decay. Constant wrong thought patterns in one's life draw demons to inhabit such a life—for example, continual criticism of others. There is a fragrance in thought, which in this case would be stinking thinking. UnChrist-like thoughts are decayed thoughts which attract and empower demons. You cannot afford to have thoughts about yourself or others that Christ does not have; otherwise, you are entertaining thoughts that war against the purposes of God.

> And be not conformed [*made to resemble; assuming the same form*] to this world: but be ye transformed [*metamorphosized, transfigured, changed*] by the renewing of your mind, that ye may prove what is that good, and acceptable, and perfect, will of God.
> —ROMANS 12:2
> (EMPHASIS MINE)

Transformation, metamorphosis, transfiguration, and change come about by the renewing of your mind. This is necessary for you to prove the good, acceptable, and perfect will of God by living the will of God and manifesting its fruit in your life. So, when the fruit of God's acceptable will is not manifesting in your life, it means that you do not have a renewed mind, and that you are not being transformed to the image of Christ. How do you know that your mind is renewed? The answer is when your thoughts are the same as the Word of God pertaining to any matter. Renewal of the mind by the Word of God leads to transformation. The transformed state, by the renewal of your mind, gives you power and authority to forbid what is not allowed in heaven and to permit only what heaven permits in your life. In the prayer that Jesus taught His disciples, He said, "Thy will be done on earth as it is in heaven." How do you know what is in heaven in order to effect it on Earth? The Word of God tells you. How do you know what obtains in the presence of God? Through your renewed mind. The renewed mind sees from heaven to Earth. On the Mount of Transfiguration, Jesus revealed and reflected the reality of another kingdom. That is what the renewed mind does. The renewed mind is in conjunction with heaven's realities. Your destination is heaven, but your responsibility is to bring heaven to Earth. Heaven is filled with absolute faith in God.

The renewed mind is a transformed person, and a transformed person transforms things. At the marriage in Cana, Jesus Christ changed water into wine because that was what was needed at that time in that situation in that marriage. What is needed in your life? In an adverse situation, the renewed mind thinks about nothing else except the Word of God for that situation. If your child is acting up, you are not going to be saying what the devil is showing you, but the first question that should go through your mind is, "What does the Word of God say about this situation?" You will speak what the Word of God says, and as you do this, it transforms the situation because you are a transformer.

First Thessalonians 5:5–6 says that as children of light and of the day, we need to be vigilant and sober. It is not someone else that will be vigilant over your life for you. You need to do this for yourself—being vigilant with the Word of God and being sober. The word *sober* can also be called *circumspect* which means cautious, prudent, watchful on all sides; carefully examining all the circumstances that may affect a determination; wisely avoiding errors and evil; and selecting the best means to accomplish a purpose. When your mind is renewed, regardless of what circumstance you are in, you are vigilant and sober to test the situation with the Word of God. If it is in line with the Word of God, you receive it. However, if it is contrary to the Word of God, you reject it and speak into that situation what the Word of God says it should be. The renewed mind only permits what God has said about your life or a particular situation.

> Let this mind be in you, which was also in Christ Jesus.
> —PHILIPPIANS 2:5

The word *let* in this verse means to allow the mind of Christ to be in you. This also means that you can disallow or refuse it. It is one thing to be given something, but it is another thing to receive it and use it. God has given you the mind of Christ, so receive it, embrace it, and work with it. Do all things by it. It was the mind that Christ had that led Him to be humble and obedient to every Word of His Father, up to His death on the cross. As a result of this, God has highly exalted Jesus Christ above every principality, power, and dominion; and His name is above every name in this age and the age to come. Every knee will bow to Jesus, and every tongue shall confess that He is Lord (Phil. 2:9–11). When you allow the mind of Christ to rule and reign in your life, then you will get the same results that Christ had. When you operate with the mind of Christ, having the emotions, will, and thoughts of Christ, then you will do the actions of Christ, speak the Words of Christ, and relate to people the way Christ would, etc. You will be humble and always obedient to God's Word, no matter the situation or circumstance.

With the mind of Christ, there is no love for or enticement toward sin or anything contrary to the Word of God. There is no struggle to read the Word or to spend time in prayer and worship. You make the right choices and decisions because you are not after your own will, but God's will. The mind of Christ does not think "my will," but "What is God's will for me?" or "What is God's will in this situation?" The mind of Christ is in perfect alignment with God's will at all times. Jesus never went out of God's will, so He was never tripped by the Pharisees, Sadducees, and scribes, even though they tried. The mind of Christ always says "Yes" to the Father and lives for the Father. There is no guile in the mind of Christ. Jesus was never overcome by evil nor defeated by the devil. Without the mind of Christ, you cannot sit in heavenly places in Christ—the exalted place that is highly above all principalities, powers, and dominion. In this exalted place, you are more than a conqueror in Christ and, therefore, in a place of no defeat.

Scientists have proven that our DNA is not constant, but changes with our interaction with our environment and our thinking. As a man thinks in his heart, so is he (Prov. 23:7). I have seen believers' thinking patterns and attitudes change as they completely yield to the Word of God in adverse situations and do exactly what the Word of God says, trusting God every step of the way. It is our godly responses to adversities that mold and transform us to the image of Christ and thus make us His savor. Let me share some examples.

DIVORCE

This person has forgiven herself and her ex-spouse, given the situation to God, and received healing from Him. This has not occurred in one day, but over a period of time as she yielded to God and His Word. She now knows that she has to move on with life in the purposes of God. She knows that you are not formed by your failures, but by the Word of God that delivered you from those failures. This person now rejoices in the Lord and thanks God for each day she is blessed with and for the people that He has brought into her life that she can fellowship with. She rejoices to see healthy marriages, and when she sees those that are getting sour, she prays for them. Whenever she gets an opportunity, she gives an encouraging word. She now appreciates God-given relationships, nurturing and guarding them with God's love. The healing from inside has made this person tender, and she does not compromise the Word of God. She has seen that during shaking and seeming darkness, one has to continue agreeing with the future God has spoken. So, when situations happen in other people's lives, she is not judgmental, knowing the complexities of life. While others are busy giving their opinions, all she can think of is restoration to the lives involved; she prays for them and sees how she can be a blessing to them.

LOSS OF A CHILD OR A LOVED ONE

This person has experienced the pain of loss, especially when it was unexpected. She has gone through the stage of "Why me?" "Did I do something wrong, or was there something I should have done that I did not do?" to the stage of "God, I trust You, and I know that You love me." She has come to know that there is promise and purpose in pain and that God wants you to trust Him and function through the pain. So, when someone in the sphere of her life experiences a loss, she can empathize with that person. When the immediate grieving period is over and the visitors have stopped coming, she persists in giving a helping hand, praying for the person who suffered a loss, and just being there for her / him. Sometimes it is a scripture shared. Sometimes it is delivering a home-cooked meal or getting groceries for the individual. She comforts with the same comfort that Christ comforted her in her loss, all the time emphasizing the love of Christ. This person becomes a trusted friend in the time of loss.

REJECTION

A person who has been rejected builds walls around himself in order to avoid being hurt again by others. He does not know how to receive love from others or give love to others. Anytime you try to touch this person with the love of God, it is as if you have been pricked by thorns. However, he has now stopped blaming the whole world for his problems and has yielded to the love of Christ at the cross and received healing for his wounds. Through the love of Christ, he releases all who have rejected him, even when they have not asked him for forgiveness. In forgiving them, he has experienced freedom in Christ and is now able to enjoy life once again. He is no longer bound to his past and knows that he is a son of God, accepted in the beloved.

This person easily discerns those who have been rejected and have not received their healing; he is patient with them even when they are unseeingly rude. Others might see them as uncultured or brash in their attitude, but this person sees the root problem and the bondage these individuals are in. He goes the extra mile to see that these individuals get their breakthrough and freedom through the power of Christ. He is careful when handling people, especially the people of God, and does not have a religious spirit. This person exudes the love of Christ because he knows that everyone needs to be loved.

BETRAYAL

Those who have been betrayed are usually bound by unforgiveness and bitterness. You only use the word *betrayal* when it is done by a loved one or friend rather than an enemy. That is why it hurts so badly. This person no longer trusts anyone and is very apprehensive. As a result, he lies, so that you do not really know what is happening in his life. However, this individual has now been delivered from the hurts of betrayal. He has come to know the saving power of Christ; even in that situation of betrayal, he sees that it was Christ who preserved his life. He no longer fights for himself, but gives the battle to the Lord in prayer. He no longer depends on his own strength, but on the strength of the Lord. He no longer tries to justify himself to others, but allows God to do so. He now knows what it means to live a life surrendered to the lordship of Christ. He now walks in the wisdom of God. This is someone who consciously walks in the fear of God because he knows that is where his preservation lies. He becomes a good counselor to those experiencing betrayal and tells them that instead of focusing on the hurt, they should focus on the goodness of God. He knows that no weapon formed against a child of God shall prosper! He walks in the joy of the Lord, and the joy of the Lord is his strength.

LOSS OF JOB OR HOUSE

This person has experienced either of these or both. He has gone through hard times and has seen his company change quickly as his economic status deteriorated. He has learned to hold on to Jesus because that is all he had left, and he has seen the Lord prove Himself in his situation over and over again. The Lord has brought him through. He has formed a special relationship with Jehovah Jireh and knows that God is truly a provider. God makes something out of nothing. When someone around him is in a similar situation, he is able to minister to the person. While others are asking about the progress in the person's job search, reassuring him with mere words or quick prayers, this person slips an envelope with money into the needy person's hands and quickly moves away. Occasionally, he turns up to the house with groceries or takes the family out for a treat or a meal.

> Be sober, be vigilant; because your adversary the devil, as a roaring lion, walketh about, seeking whom he may devour: Whom resist stedfast in the faith, knowing that the same afflictions are accomplished in your brethren that are in the world.
>
> —1 PETER 5:8–9

Just as we have a common Savior, Jesus Christ, we also have a common adversary. First Peter 5:8 tells us who our adversary is: the devil. He is not a roaring lion, but is as a roaring lion because the noise he creates in your life causes you to fear. He seeks who he can devour because he knows that it is not everyone he can devour. The Greek word for *devour* is *katapinō* which means to drink down, gulp entirely, devour, or swallow. When Lot refused God's perfect will for him and his family to flee Sodom and escape to the mountain (Gen. 19:17–18), he went to a city called Zoar. *Zoar* means small, little, or insignificant.[3] This city was originally called *Bela* which means destruction, swallower, or devourer.[4] Sometimes, it is the seemingly little things that are out of the will of God that the devil uses to swallow believers. The devil wants to swallow you by causing you to make the wrong choices. God has given each one of us willpower to make our choices. Your choices create your circumstances. What you want is God's perfect will for you and not His permissive will. God's perfect will for you is His Word. Therefore, His perfect will exactly conforms to His Word and disallows and prohibits everything contrary. God's way is perfect (2 Sam. 22:31), and His will is perfect.

> But whoso looketh into the perfect law of liberty, and continueth therein, he being not a forgetful hearer, but a doer of the work, this man shall be blessed in his deed.
> —JAMES 1:25

God's Word is the perfect law of liberty, and we are to look into it. Looking into the Word of God entails researching it, studying it in depth under the guidance of the Holy Spirit, and attentively hearing it with understanding so we are not forgetful hearers. Therein, we are mindful to do it and are blessed in whatever we do. The Word of God that is understood cannot be stolen from our hearts by the devil. Liberty means the state of being free from conditions that limit one's actions. Liberty cannot be found outside the Word of God. Your steps are ordered in His Word (Ps. 119:133). Outside the Word is bondage. It is the truth of the Word that ensures freedom for the believer. Where the Spirit of the Lord is, there is liberty, and the Word of God is Spirit and life. You cannot kill spirit, and the life in the Word is the light of men.

The devil cannot devour the believer who has a renewed mind because he is transfigured or transformed. Should we be scared because the devil is walking about as a roaring lion? No. We are to resist him steadfastly in the faith with a renewed mind and not with our personal reasoning, knowing that similar trials and afflictions are happening to other believers in the world (1 Pet. 5:9). This is not something passive, but active—so, you have to be actively engaged.

> Wherefore gird up the loins of your mind, be sober, and hope to the end for the grace that is to be brought unto you at the revelation of Jesus Christ.
> —1 PETER 1:13

To *gird up* means tighten or gather together. To gird up the loins of your mind means to strengthen the procreativity of your mind, and this is done with the Word of God. You have to be determined that the Word of God will stay in your mind. Keep on reading the Word of God till you think the Word. The time you spend watching soap operas or continually tuning in to the radio or television to hear about events going on in the world should be spent reading the Word of God. Some of us can recount in detail the last episode of our favorite soap opera, while others can mime every worldly song you can think of, but they cannot recite the Word of God. You do not use one hand to gird up, but two. When you gird up the loins of your mind with the Word of God, you use everything in you to do this, and your imagination comes in line with the Word of God. Your imagination becomes sanctified. A woman cannot have a girded-up mind and imagine that she is getting married to a married man because that is someone else's husband, and this imagination is contrary to the Word of God. It is only a mind that is girded up with the Word of God that can endure in truth till Jesus comes back again.

Your will is not to conform to God's will like two wills aligning; only His will should exist in your life. This means that all the time you are to seek to do God's will. This is consecration. Abandon your will and follow His will.

> For it is God which worketh in you both to will and to do of his good pleasure.
> —Philippians 2:13

In the prayer that Jesus taught His disciples, He said, "Thy will be done in earth as it is in heaven" (Matt. 6:10). In heaven, there is only one will that is done, and it is God's will! Jesus always did God's will and not His (John 5:30). The Bible does not say our will should be conformed to His will, but that we should be conformed to the image of Jesus (Rom. 8:29) who has only one will, which is God's.

> And God spake unto Moses, and said unto him, I am the Lord: And I appeared unto Abraham, unto Isaac, and unto Jacob, by the name of God Almighty, but by my name Jehovah was I not known to them. And I have also established my covenant with them, to give them the land of Canaan, the land of their pilgrimage, wherein they were strangers. And I

have also heard the groaning of the children of
Israel, whom the Egyptians keep in bondage; and
I have remembered my covenant. Wherefore say
unto the children of Israel, I am the LORD, and I
will bring you out from under the burdens of the
Egyptians, and I will rid you out of their bondage,
and I will redeem you with a stretched out arm, and
with great judgments: And I will take you to me for
a people, and I will be to you a God: and ye shall
know that I am the LORD your God, which bringeth
you out from under the burdens of the Egyptians.
And I will bring you in unto the land, concerning
the which I did swear to give it to Abraham, to Isaac,
and to Jacob; and I will give it you for an heritage: I
am the LORD.

—EXODUS 6:2–8

If you look at what the Lord was speaking to Moses in
the above scripture, there is a common thread that runs
through. He keeps on saying "I am the Lord." God is
bringing Himself foremost to Moses. He is saying, "Do
not concentrate on what Pharaoh is doing. Do not concentrate on what he is inflicting on the people right now.
Concentrate on Me who spoke to you. I who spoke to you,
I am the Lord. I am not only God Almighty; I am the
Lord." This means there is no other Lord apart from Him.
He is the Lord. He said that their fathers knew Him by
the name of God Almighty. God Almighty in Hebrew is
El Shaddai which also means the All Sufficient One and
most powerful.[5] He said to Moses, "But I am manifesting
Myself to you as Jehovah." Jehovah means the Self-Existing
or Eternal One who keeps covenant and fulfills promises.
Have you known your Father as that?

He has not only made covenant with us through His Son Jesus Christ, but He keeps covenant and fulfills all His promises. He is not man that He should lie (Num. 23:19). We know Him as a covenant-making God, but do we know Him as a covenant keeper? The Bible says that God keeps His covenant and He does not alter the thing that has gone forth from His lips (Ps. 89:34). If you know this, then you will not be afraid when the enemy is showing you a contrary scene. It is just a scene. It must alter to what God has said. He says, "I am the Lord. I am the Lord of the Israelites. I am the Lord of Pharaoh. I am the Lord of the Egyptians. I am the Lord of all creation. I am the Lord of everything, the seen and the unseen. I am the Lord." The people of God need to get this revelation because when you know that God who is your Father is the Lord, then you will not be afraid of anyone or anything. You will not be afraid of the wiles and schemes of the devil. You will walk into your workplace knowing that your Father is the Lord. You will know that no obstacle or hindrance can remain standing before you because your Father is the Lord. He is over all things. He is the greatest! This revelation should make an imprint in your spirit. God told Moses, "When you go back to the people, say I am the Lord. When you go before Pharaoh, know that I am the Lord. He is Pharaoh, and he is seated on the throne, but I am the Lord. Pharaoh's face might not look favorable, what he says might sound nasty, what he is doing is evil, but I am the Lord. Because I am the Lord, I am the One that is going to bring you out from under this burden. I am the One who will get you out of this bondage. I will redeem you with My stretched-out arm, and I will do it with great judgments. It does not matter how many armies there are on Earth, I am the Lord! I am the One who is going to bring you out, and I am the One who is going to take you in because I am the Lord. What I am going to give you is going to be an inheritance. It is going to be for you, your children, and your children's children long after you have gone. Nobody can take it from you because I am the Lord." The Lord is Master, supreme in authority and power, and all things belong to Him.

David as a young man got this revelation. That is why during his confrontation with Goliath, he could run toward him because he knew that his God, Jehovah, is the Lord. The world is trying to silence believers, but we are the ones that have to declare who God is because we are the ones who know Him. Do you know that you and I have a heritage in God and our access to that heritage is Jesus Christ? When you know that the One who has given you that heritage is the Lord, you will not move your ground. You will lay claim on the promises of God and possess your possession because He is the Lord and He is Lord of all.

> And the LORD said unto Moses, See, I have made
> thee a god to Pharaoh: and Aaron thy brother shall
> be thy prophet.
> —EXODUS 7:1

Once you get the revelation that your God, Jehovah, is the Lord, then you will not see the obstacle before you as an obstacle. You will not see the mountain before you as a mountain, but you will see that you are god of the mountain. Jehovah the Lord was the one sending Moses as His representative to Pharaoh; therefore, what Moses was going to do before Pharaoh was not to be done in his own merit. Because God was sending Moses to Pharaoh as His representative, he was going as god before Pharaoh. *Moses was made a god to Pharaoh.* How did God do this? By His Word—and by Moses perceiving who God is and believing that He is the Lord. It therefore meant that whatever Pharaoh did or said to Moses would not prevail, but whatever Moses spoke to Pharaoh must come to pass. Pharaoh brought his magicians, but what Moses did swallowed up whatever the magicians conjured because before Pharaoh, Moses was a god. It is time we started walking in this knowledge that changes our perception of difficulties in our lives. The difficulty is not there to kill you. It is there to help you rise to the level that God has ordained. The question is, "Are you going about doing your own thing, or are you doing what God has called you to?" When you are doing what God has called you to and something comes to try to block you, you are a god to that thing because your God is the Lord, and it is His assignment that you are on.

> I, the Most High God, say that all of you are gods
> and also my own children. But you will die, just like
> everyone else, including powerful rulers.
> —PSALM 82:6–7, CEV

> Jesus answered them, "Is it not written in your Law,
> 'I said, you are gods'?"
> —JOHN 10:34, ESV

Moses was going before Pharaoh not in the name of Moses, but in the name of the Lord. Remember, Moses was raised in Pharaoh's palace. He could have easily gotten into logical thinking and said, "Well, you know the Lord chose me because I am the most educated amongst the Israelites. I have had special training and can come before

Pharaoh. I know the layout of the palace and know how to
get to him. I know the protocol. God chose me because I
am the right person." Do you know he could have fallen
into that thinking? Thank God he did not. Sometimes we
fall into that thinking when the Lord chooses us to do a
job. We start thinking logically, "I am very well trained to
do this. I am a professional teacher, so it is not a coincidence that I am teaching in the church." You will fall on
your face with such thinking. You have to know that it is
Jehovah, the One who is the Lord of all, who has commissioned you. When you have this revelation, you will
be able to run and finish the race. On the path of the race,
there are obstacles. Have you ever watched an obstacle
race? The obstacles are there to stop the runner. However,
the runner that will win is the one who will not allow the
obstacles to stop him. When he approaches the obstacles,
he picks up his pace in order to have momentum to go
over the obstacles. The obstacle is not there to kill you. It
is there to help you rise to who God has called you to be.
God has not called us to reduce Him but to represent Him.

The further you go in your journey in God, the greater
the obstacles. The more you come to a realization of what
God has commissioned you to do, the greater the mountain before you. You have to rise in your spirit with the
knowledge that Jehovah is Lord. You have to walk in that to
which He has called you—as an ambassador to Christ. The
Bible tells us that we are Christ's ambassadors. The Bible
doesn't say that you are Jesus' ambassador. The Bible says
that you are Christ's ambassador. You are the ambassador
of the Messiah. You are the ambassador of the Anointed
One. Whatever you are doing is in Christ's stead. So it
means that whatever you are doing, you are doing it in the

ability of the Messiah. Isn't that humbling? Some of us cry out, "Lord, why do you always bring dysfunctional people my way?" It is for you to lead them to salvation because you are Christ's ambassador. What God has put in you is for others. When you say, "Jesus Christ, You are Lord," do you know the meaning of what you're saying? He is the Lord; therefore, nothing is capable of stopping you. You are unstoppable in the task the Lord has given you. You are unstoppable, and you have to see yourself as unstoppable.

> Ye are of God, little children, and have overcome them: because greater is he that is in you, than he that is in the world. They are of the world: therefore speak they of the world, and the world heareth them. We are of God: he that knoweth God heareth us; he that is not of God heareth not us. Hereby know we the spirit of truth, and the spirit of error.
>
> —1 John 4:4–6

We are of God. That word *of* in the Greek means "origin."[6] Your origin is God. Your origin is not the devil. The born-again believer is of God. The Bible says that for the new creature, old things have passed away and all things have become new. All things are of God—all things originate from God (1 Cor. 5:17–18). We should be mindful of this: that we are of God, and therefore our walk should be god-like. If you know that you are of God, then the supernatural is the norm in your life. If your name is Judith, are you operating as Judith, or are you operating as Judith who is a new creation in Christ, who is of God? When you think of your lineage, what immediately comes to your mind? Is it your nation? Is it your family—or is it God? One of the things that the religious leaders could not stand was for Jesus to say that He was the Son of God; that is what the enemy cannot stand. The Bible calls us sons of God (Gal. 4:6). So what is your perception of yourself? The Bible says as a man thinks in his heart so is he (Prov. 23:7). Are you going to remain in the place of limitation? Or are you going to get into the realm of no limitation? You are from God, and you are of God. If you are of God, you overcome the world because greater is He who is in you than he who is in the world. He who is in you is the Lord.

> He that cometh from above is above all: he that is of the earth is earthly, and speaketh of the earth: he that cometh from heaven is above all.
> —JOHN 3:31

You are of God, you are from God, and God is from above. If you are from above, you are above all. In your daily lifestyle, how do you operate? Do you operate as somebody from the Earth or from above? Since you are above all, you are above only. You will not be beneath. Receive it in your spirit.

> And the LORD shall make thee the head, and not the tail; and thou shalt be above only, and thou shalt not be beneath; if that thou hearken unto the commandments of the LORD thy God, which I command thee this day, to observe and to do them.
> —DEUTERONOMY 28:13

You are the head and not the tail. The tail is behind, and it wags. The head is above, and it is steady. Being above only means there is no sphere of your life where you are beneath. For some of us, we are above in some areas and below in others, and our excuse is that "we are just human." Are you? You are from above. That is the Word of God.

> Blessed be the God and Father of our Lord Jesus Christ, who hath blessed us with all spiritual blessings in heavenly places in Christ.
> —Ephesians 1:3

Are heavenly places above or beneath? They are above, and in your position above, you are blessed with all spiritual blessings. When you operate from this position above, you will not be envious of your sister or brother in Christ in whatever they do because you know that from your heavenly seating, which is above, you are blessed with all spiritual blessings.

> And hath raised us up together, and made us sit together in heavenly places in Christ Jesus.
> —Ephesians 2:6

He has given us the same seating in Christ, which is above, and that is where we should be.

> To the intent that now unto the principalities and powers in heavenly places might be known by the church the manifold wisdom of God, according to the eternal purpose which he purposed in Christ Jesus our Lord: In whom we have boldness and access with confidence by the faith of him.
> —Ephesians 3:10–12

Operating from our heavenly seating, the church is to display the wisdom of God to principalities and powers so that when they see the god-like manner in which we operate, they will say, "Oh God, You were wise in allowing Jesus to go to the cross."

> Simon Peter, a servant and an apostle of Jesus Christ, to them that have obtained like precious faith with us through the righteousness of God and our Savior Jesus Christ: Grace and peace be multiplied unto you through the knowledge of God, and of Jesus our Lord, according as his divine power hath given unto us all things that pertain unto life and godliness, through the knowledge of him that hath called us to glory and virtue: Whereby are given unto us exceeding great and precious promises: that by these ye might be partakers of the divine nature, having escaped the corruption that is in the world through lust.
>
> —2 PETER 1:1–4

The power of God has given us all things that pertain to life and godliness through the knowledge of Him that has called us to glory and virtue. The One who is eternal, who keeps covenant and fulfills promises is He who has given us exceedingly great and precious promises. Have you seen somebody promise what he or she is not able to do? Sadly, there are people like that. They cannot even feed themselves, and they promise to buy you a house. Our God is not like that. Our God is Lord of all. He is the owner and Creator of all things, and by His valuable promises, we will be partakers of His nature. We are to be partakers of the divine nature of God, having escaped the corruption that is in the world through lust. We have escaped it through Christ Jesus.

When you hear the word *escape,* the picture that comes

to your mind is a close shave, something that almost got you. Have you heard somebody say, "Oh you know, I just escaped death." It was so near; it almost happened. That is how the Lord has snatched us from the path of corruption and death. He snatched us not that we might be an end unto ourselves, but that we might partake of His divine nature. You know what He calls you? He calls you *son*. Sons are like their fathers. Take a look at your children. You know some of their idiosyncrasies, and you wonder where they got them from. Look at yourself. However, our Father is perfect. He has given us these promises, and He has the ability to fulfill—not some, but all of them. He says these promises are exceeding great and precious (according to God's standard and not your standard) so that we can, through them, partake of His divine nature. That is why you can say, "It is no longer I who lives, but Christ who lives through me." So when you start saying, "What is my life coming to?" My question to you is, "Are you still holding on to your life?" You are supposed to be walking in the divine nature of God which no demon from hell can snuff out.

Jesus knew who He was. He said, "I know where I come from, and I know where I am going to. Nobody takes My life. I lay it down, and the One who is Lord, My Father, has given Me power to pick it up again." Do you know where you come from? Are you still looking at your passport to know where you come from? Do you know you are from above? If you know you are from above, whatever color your passport bears will be no hindrance to your walk of destiny in God. When you know that you are from above, wherever you go, you go in the name of Lord, in the name of the One who is above—and who is above all. When you know that you are from above, you will no longer tolerate vices in your life. The old man is dead. The earthy has gone back to the earthy when Christ died and went into the tomb. As He rose, you have risen in Him and now walk in divine nature through taking possession of the exceeding great and precious promises of God through Christ.

BROW GUARD
ON THE FOREHEAD

When the Roman soldier's helmet was properly worn on his head, the brow guard laid squarely on his forehead. In God's army, you go into spiritual warfare fully consecrated to God. Engraved in a gold plate on the forefront of the high priest's miter were the words "Holiness to the Lord." He wore this on his forehead continually (Exod. 28:38). The first thing the devil should see in your life is holiness, which he cannot stand, and so he has to flee. You do not go into warfare against the devil when you are on his side. God has not called you unto uncleanliness, but unto holiness (1 Thess. 4:7). As a soldier in God's army, you stand on holy ground, and what you perceive is through His holiness and purity.

You need to ask the Father to give you an understanding of holiness so that He and His Word are your standard for holiness and not any human being on Earth. God is holy and nothing that defiles, commits abominations, or practices falsehood shall enter into the holy city Jerusalem, which descends from God out of heaven (Rev. 21:27). Ask the Father to cleanse you in every area of your life so that holiness becomes your lifestyle. Your walk, thoughts, and responses to people should be holy. Jesus was holy in everything He did. Though He was surrounded by so much evil, He remained holy. God has given Him to us as our Savior and as an example of how to walk on planet Earth. We need to be delivered from the spirit of compromise and everything that makes us stray from God's way. God is our Father; we are to be like Him, for we are His children. His seed is in us—that holy seed. Our spiritual wombs need to be able to conceive and carry that which is holy so that everything that is birthed from us is holy. It emanates from God's throne and not from us. We cannot work out holiness, but it is our total dependence on God through the Holy Spirit, abiding in Him and His Word, that brings holiness. We need to continually submit and cooperate with the Holy Spirit. Right now, thank the Holy Spirit for abiding with you, for being patient with you, and for doing our Father's bidding in your life.

> As an adamant harder than flint have I made thy forehead: fear them not, neither be dismayed at their looks, though they be a rebellious house.
> —EZEKIEL 3:9

> For the Lord GOD will help me; therefore shall I not be confounded: therefore have I set my face like a flint, and I know that I shall not be ashamed.
> —ISAIAH 50:7

You have to set your face like flint to do the work of God and finish it. Flint is a hard stone or rock, so it is not impressible. To impress means to imprint, stamp, or make a mark on something by pressure—like impressing a coin with a figure of a man's head. Do not yield to pressure; do not allow suffering or any contrary situation make its impress or stamp on you. Refuse to allow it to fix deep in you so as to impress your mind or memory; otherwise, it alters your thinking from the thoughts of God about you and your situation.

EMBOSSED EYEBROWS

Let your eyes look right on [with fixed purpose], and let your gaze be straight before you.
—PROVERBS 4:25, AMP

Keep your eyes straight ahead; ignore all sideshow distractions.
—PROVERBS 4:25, THE MESSAGE

Saints of God, ignore all sideshows—gossip, covetousness, overeating, etc., which are distractions that emanate from the world. If you are married, ignore all sideshows of adultery. If you are single, keep your vessel in purity and ignore all sideshows of fornication. Sideshows distract you from walking holy. Once you move out of the holy path, you are on the enemy's ground, and he will floor you. Love God more than the sideshows.

PROJECTING EAR GUARDS

These are embossed areas on the helmet above the ear lobes to protect the ears. Mind what you hear. What you hear will either bring faith or fear into your heart. What are you hearing? It has to be guarded. You do not just allow garbage such as gossip, slander, subversion, scorn, and unhealthy criticism into your ears. You might say, "Oh, they brought the story to where I was seated." My response to you is, "Why did you not get up from the chair and walk away from the gossip? Were you stuck to the chair?" When people are talking garbage and you walk into the room, they should shut up because they know that you will not receive it. Faith comes not by hearing garbage, but by hearing the Word of God.

In 1 Samuel 17:44, Goliath spoke words to instill fear in David. David did not receive this, as shown by his response. Do not receive anything from the devil! David's focus was on the victory God was about to give him and the Israelite army. David said to Goliath (paraphrased), "You come to me in your own strength, but I come to you in the name of the Lord of hosts, Jehovah Sabaoth."

> Is it not the task of the ear to discriminate between [wise and unwise] words, just as the mouth distinguishes [between desirable and undesirable] food?
> —JOB 12:11, AMP

You are responsible for what you hear. Do not allow the clutter and noise of situations in your life get into you and deafen your ears, preventing you from hearing God. Your ears should hear and understand (Job 13:1). We should be people of understanding because the spirit of understanding is in us (Isa. 11:1).The anointing of the Holy Spirit quickens our spiritual understanding. The Holy Spirit gave Jesus quick understanding in the fear of God (Isa. 11:3). David prayed that the Lord would give his son Solomon wisdom and understanding so that he would keep the law of God. When we understand that the Word of God is abundant life, we will keep it and also understand that everything contrary to the Word is death. You have got to know who you are obeying. Are you obeying God's voice or the devil's voice? His sheep know Him and His voice, and no other voice will they listen to. They know His voice and follow Him (John 10:4–5, 27). You know God's voice from intimacy with Him. Obey everything the Lord speaks to you. Obey His voice.

> But if thou shalt indeed obey his voice, and do all
> that I speak; then I will be an enemy unto thine ene-
> mies, and an adversary unto thine adversaries.
>
> —EXODUS 23:22

CHEEK AND JAW GUARDS

Proverbs 11:12 tells us that a man of understanding holds his peace. You do not have to be a tattler. Others do not always have to hear your opinion about everything. When you hold your tongue, you hold onto your peace, and you are not drawn into unnecessary battles or battles that are not yours. The reason some people are overwhelmed is that they have engaged in battles that are not primarily theirs. We only engage in battles that are ours—that God has anointed us to take on. There are times you will want to fight for a cause, and the Lord will say, "Shut up. Keep quiet."

> Put away from thee a froward mouth, and perverse
> lips put far from thee.
>
> —PROVERBS 4:24

A forward mouth is an ungovernable mouth. Have you ever met someone who cannot stop talking, even when what he is saying does not make sense or have any relation to the subject at hand? Such a person has a need to constantly hear his voice. Perverse lips are lips that distort what is right. I like the way *The Message Bible* puts it.

> Don't talk out of both sides of your mouth; avoid careless banter, white lies, and gossip.
> —PROVERBS 4:24, THE MESSAGE

You guard what you speak by the Word of God. That is why the cheek and the jaw guards are present.

> But as he which hath called you is holy, so be ye holy in all manner of conversation; because it is written, Be ye holy; for I am holy.
> —1 PETER 1:15–16

Your conversation should be holy, not only when you are in church, but also when you are in the workplace. Some believers try so hard to sound like the world by using the same language. You are either saved or ensnared by the words of your mouth. Therefore, use your mouth to confess your salvation (deliverance). Say what the Word of God says.

Your thought process is directly related to that which you see as most precious to you. What is most precious to you? The Lord should be the most precious to you. Some of us have made the choice of what is most precious based on what we see with our eyes, but the Lord, who is unseen with our physical eyes, is the most precious. What is most precious to you consumes you day and night; it is magnified in your thoughts and fills your speech. What or who do you talk mostly about? Is it about the world events, your finances, members of your family, your plans and ambitions, your future, other people, your relationships, etc.? Whatever or whoever it is, that is where your heart is because from the abundance of the heart, the mouth speaks.

Do you not know that you will be judged for every idle word you speak? For those that fear the Lord and talk about Him, their names are written in a book (Mal. 3:16). The times are short, and the coming back of the Lord Jesus Christ is nearer than anyone of us might care to think. It is time for you to start talking about the Lord. Talk about Him in the morning, afternoon, evening, and night seasons of your life. The very thought of the Lord should consume you. It is what you talk about that holds your focus. The more you talk about the Lord, the more you are focused on Him. When your heart dwells on the Lord and you talk about Him, you begin to be sensitive to things in the Spirit and are able to identify God's hand in situations. You begin to see God in everything around you. Let us look at the Lord's instruction to the Israelites through Moses in Deuteronomy 6:6–7.

> And these words, which I command thee this day,
> shall be in thine heart: And thou shalt teach them
> diligently unto thy children, and shalt talk of them
> when thou sittest in thine house, and when thou
> walkest by the way, and when thou liest down, and
> when thou risest up.

Where the Lord is being talked about, an environment is created wherein the devil cannot stay. This is because he cannot stand anyone talking about the Lord. That is why the devil wants you to talk continually about your problems. In so doing, you are talking about him. Who will you allow to take your focus? The person you allow to take your focus is the one you worship. Worship involves giving your time and attention to something or someone. It is time that the saints of God become wise. We should not only walk in knowledge, but also in wisdom. It is time for us to change the way we talk. Some people talk about everything else, except the Lord. We should talk about the Lord seven days a week. That is why He has given us His Word. His Word is for us to talk about! God's Word is nigh in our mouths, but we need to give attention to it to speak it forth. We create the milieu that we live and work in. Have you forgotten that everything was created by the spoken Word? What are you creating? You are living now in what you spoke years ago.

One day while we were in worship in the church and singing over and over again that we love Jesus, I saw a glimpse of what happens when we unashamedly speak the love of Jesus, when we are not ashamed to say that we love Him. What I saw in the spirit were great waves of the sea just rolling and rolling and rolling on our behalf with each stanza of saying that we love Jesus. That is how the power of God moves on our behalf as we unashamedly express our love for Him. When you express your love for Him, you bring yourself into a place of holy habitation because God is love. You bring yourself into a place where the enemy cannot tread because one thing the enemy does not have is love. When you walk in hatred, you are walking in defeat because you are walking in the territory of the enemy. He will floor you all the time when you are in his territory. The Lord wants us to walk in love. Refuse the offence that the enemy is giving you as bait. When offence comes your way, say, "I refuse you." The Bible in Romans 13:8 says that we should owe all people love, meaning that we love and keep on loving all people, and this fulfills the law of God. When we keep on loving, we ensure that we are in the place of victory.

John 3:16 says that God so loved the world that He gave His only begotten Son, that whosoever believes in Him should not perish, but have everlasting life. It is God's love that gave us victory, and that love still governs the life of a believer. The laws of God never change and can never change because He never does. So, you must refuse offence. The enemy may hand offence to you ten times a day, but each time as he hands it to you, refuse it. It is only when you receive offence that it can work in your life, thereby robbing you of God's promises. You cannot stop the devil from handing offence to you, but you can stop yourself from receiving it. When you dwell in the place of love, no demon spirit can influence you because where there is love, there is God. So, on a daily basis, we have to learn to exercise speaking our love for God. When you dwell in love, you dwell in God, and you are thus indestructible.

Do you not know that the relationship between us and Jesus is a love relationship between lovers? With God the Father, it is a Father-child relationship in which we express our love for Him as our Father and also receive His love. With Jesus, who is the brightness of God's glory and the express image of His person (Heb. 1:3), it is a love relationship between the bridegroom and His bride. We need to express our love for Him, even as He expressed his love for us on the cross. What you saw on the cross was love. In a relationship between a bridegroom and a bride, there is an exchange of love. He has shown us His. Where is ours for Him? It does not hurt when we just take some seconds between our chores of the day to say, "Jesus, I love You.

Jesus, I love You." Depression will flee and despondency will go. Fear cannot remain where love is. When you constantly stay in the place of love, fear has to flee. Perfect love casts out fear (1 John 4:18). Agape, the God-kind of love, never fails (1 Cor. 13:8). The word *fail* in Greek is *ekpíptō,* which means to drop away or specifically be driven out of one's course.[7] Nothing can push the God-kind of love out of the course of your life when you have it. The believer who has this love never fails. Whatever we do through the love of God never fails. God is eternal, and anything of His is eternal. When we operate in His love, we are operating in the realm of eternity. So, let us be people of love.

> He that hath my commandments, and keepeth them, he it is that loveth me: and he that loveth me shall be loved of my Father, and I will love him, and will manifest myself to him. Judas saith unto him, not Iscariot, Lord, how is it that thou wilt manifest thyself unto us, and not unto the world? Jesus answered and said unto him, If a man love me, he will keep my words: and my Father will love him, and we will come unto him, and make our abode with him.
> —JOHN 14:21–23

> For I have not spoken of myself; but the Father which sent me, he gave me a commandment, what I should say, and what I should speak. And I know that his commandment is life everlasting: whatsoever I speak therefore, even as the Father said unto me, so I speak.
> —JOHN 12:49–50

The word *command* means to tell (someone) to do something with the right or authority to be obeyed. A commandment is a command that is law, which in this case is God's law. Whatsoever Jesus therefore speaks is as the Father has commanded Him, which is eternal life. That is why Jesus said in John 6:63, "The words that I speak to you, they are spirit (*the Spirit quickens or gives life*) and life (*the God-kind of life*)." Peter realized this, and that is why in John 6:68, he said that Jesus has the words of eternal life. When you speak the Word of God, you speak eternal life which is a commandment from God with God's authority to be obeyed. You have eternal life because you have received Jesus Christ as your Lord and Savior and He lives in you, but you exercise the commandment of eternal life by speaking God's Word.

> Death [*ruin*]and life [Hebrew: *Chay* from root word *chayah* which means to give life] are in the power of the tongue: and they that love it shall eat the fruit thereof.
>
> —PROVERBS 18:21
> (EMPHASIS MINE)

> Thou hast proved mine heart; thou hast visited me in the night; thou hast tried me, and shalt find nothing; I am purposed that my mouth shall not transgress.
>
> —PSALM 17:3

You need to use your mouth to praise the Lord. Praise is a lifestyle and gives God the rightful place in your life. Praise stills the enemy and avenger (Ps. 8:2). You need to train your tongue to praise God. Your tongue directs your life by what you say. Your praise gives voice to celebrating, acknowledging, and glorifying God who inhabits the praises of His people (Ps. 22:3).

> Let the saints be joyful in glory: let them sing aloud upon their beds. Let the high praises of God be in their mouth, and a two-edged sword in their hand; to execute vengeance upon the heathen, and punishments upon the people; to bind their kings with chains, and their nobles with fetters of iron; to execute upon them the judgment written: this honour have all his saints. Praise ye the LORD.
>
> —PSALM 149:5–9

We are to give God thanks in everything (1 Thess. 5:18). We pass through His gates by thanksgiving and enter God's courts with praise (Ps. 100:4). We come into the presence of God with thanksgiving and praise. Where His presence is, His power is too. As long as you continually give God thanks and praise, you have continual access to His presence and therefore His power.

Angels hearken unto the voice of His Word (Ps. 103:20). This is the voice of the Word of faith which emanates from hearing and believing the Word of God and acting on it. There is an assignment in your voice. The question is, "Is it faith or fear?" Demons hearken to the voice of fear, and Job is a witness of this.

> For sighing has become my daily food; my groans pour out like water. What I feared has come upon me; what I dreaded has happened to me.
>
> —JOB 3:24–25, NIV

That which the woman with the issue of blood for twelve years said in faith came to pass (Mark 5:27–29). The uncertainty she had whether she could touch Jesus' clothes was overcome by what she confessed and heard herself say which nurtured her faith for her healing. It is the spoken Word released that performs and empowers. What David said to Goliath in faith in God came to pass (1 Sam. 17:46, 49–51). The Word of God mixed with faith profits us (Heb. 4:2). Instead of only giving your children instructions, speak faith-filled words over them. Rather than saying, "You disobedient child," say, "You are an obedient child who honors his parents. Thank God for an excellent spirit in my child." Keep on speaking faith-filled words till you see a manifestation of what you have spoken. We believe; therefore, we speak (2 Cor. 4:13). Pray your child into his destiny. The voice of faith is the voice of redemption because it rescues the redemptive purpose of a person, people group, or institution. The voice of unbelief robs. When you speak the Word of God, you are speaking light into the situation and darkness cannot seize upon the Word, keep it down, put it out, absorb it, or overpower it.

God has given us desires, but it is our business to follow up such desires to fruition. Desire is an emotion or excitement of the mind directed to the attainment or possession of an object from which pleasure, sensual, intellectual or spiritual is expected; a passion excited by the love of something and directed toward its attainment or possession. Desire is directed at the obtainable; therefore, if the Lord has given you a desire, it is obtainable. What we generally think is that we are to speak about our desires to bring them to pass. We have to speak *to* our desires. We seem to have the wrong notion that the proof of something being our desire is that the manifestation will be smooth sailing. We forget that as long as it is a God-given desire, the enemy will want to kick against it. We have to establish, appoint, and bring the manifestation of our desires to pass by speaking the Word of the Lord to the desires to bring them into the earthly realm.

NECK GUARD

At the back of the helmet is a projection which protects the neck. This is called the neck guard. Without the neck guard, the soldier's neck would be cut by the enemy, and so the soldier would be beheaded and lose his life. You cannot afford to be stiff necked or harden your neck with obstinacy through disobedience to God because it incurs His wrath. Your neck needs to be supple and able to move in any direction that He leads you.

> He who, being often reproved, hardens his neck shall suddenly be destroyed—and that without remedy.
> —PROVERBS 29:1, AMP

CROSSBARS

At the dome of the helmet was a crossbar. The ability of the Dacian falx, a two handed sickle-like sword, to reach over the Roman shield and pierce the helmet like a can opener, forced the Romans to come up with a counter-measure. This was in the form of two brass or iron bars riveted crosswise across the helmet skull. Later on, they made cross braces. Therefore, there was a cross at the dome of the helmet. This provided double thickness of metal at the critical point of the helmet to protect the soldier's head. When the enemy tried to use the Dacian falx on the helmet, the cross would not allow the helmet to be cut open. This is how great your salvation is. It is able to cover and protect you from the enemy. When you walk in the full knowledge of your salvation, it is impenetrable to the onslaught, schemes, and devices of the devil. So, your mind is protected. You need to put on, as a helmet, the hope and confident expectation of salvation.

> For the preaching of the cross is to them that perish foolishness; but unto us which are saved it is the power of God.
> —1 CORINTHIANS 1:18

The Cross is the crux of your salvation. That is where it was finished. Your redemption is finished. Your salvation is finished. What Jesus did on the cross is not to be continued; it is finished. You might be going through some issues now, but you better start speaking to yourself, "It is finished." Whatever difficulty you are in, God saw it before you were formed in your mother's womb, and He prepared His salvation, through Jesus Christ, for you. You are covered in the day of battle by God's salvation. The Cross is the center of our faith. It is the *dunamis* or miraculous power of God to the believer. Whatever situation you find yourself in, you can take it to the Cross and get your deliverance.

CREST

At the vertex of some helmets, there was a crest of hair or feathers. Not all the soldiers in the army wore this type of helmet. Only the centurions and other officers wore crests on their helmets. This was so that their men could see them and follow them into battle. The crest was usually red. We go into battle through the blood of Jesus because it wrought our covenant with God, and the enemy does not have an antidote to the blood. The blood of Jesus stays the hand of the destroyer and causes him to pass over.

> In whom we have redemption [*ransom in full; nothing more to be paid*] through [*channel of an act*] his blood, the forgiveness of sins, according to the riches [*fullness, abundance*] of his grace [*not according to our own earthly standard*].
>
> —EPHESIANS 1:7
> (EMPHASIS MINE)

Whatever sin is in your life, through Jesus' blood, you can have forgiveness for. One of the ploys of the devil is to tell you that your sin is too great to be forgiven. The blood of Jesus is greater than your sin, so it is able to cleanse you. If you confess your sins, God is faithful and just to forgive you and cleanse you from all unrighteousness (1 John 1:9). Come to the fountain of the blood of Jesus and receive forgiveness for your sins. Where is this fountain? At the Cross of Jesus. On the cross, Jesus bled from all points— from the crown of His head to the soles of His feet.

> In that day there shall be a fountain opened to the house of David and to the inhabitants of Jerusalem for sin and for uncleanness [*rejection, impurity, filthiness*].
>
> —ZECHARIAH 13:1
> (EMPHASIS MINE)

> I am poured out [*spilled forth, to expend life*] like
> water, and all my bones are out of joint: my heart is
> like wax; it is melted in the midst of my bowels.
>
> —PSALM 22:14
> (EMPHASIS MINE)

When you pour out water, do you think of taking it
back? No, and you cannot take it back even if you tried.
That is how Jesus has poured out His blood for us; He is
not taking it back.

> For the life of the flesh is in the blood: and I have
> given it to you upon the altar to make an atonement
> for your souls: for it is the blood that maketh an
> atonement for the soul.
>
> —LEVITICUS 17:11

Since the life of the flesh is in the blood, Jesus poured
out His life for us. Are you ready to receive His life and
live it?

> Whereupon neither the first testament was dedi-
> cated without blood. For when Moses had spoken
> every precept to all the people according to the law,
> he took the blood of calves and of goats, with water,
> and scarlet wool, and hyssop, and sprinkled both the
> book, and all the people, saying, This is the blood
> of the testament which God hath enjoined unto
> you. Moreover he sprinkled with blood both the
> tabernacle, and all the vessels of the ministry. And
> almost all things are by the law purged [*cleansed,
> purified*] with blood; and without shedding of blood

is no remission [*freedom, pardon, deliverance, for-giveness, liberty*].

—HEBREWS 9:18–22

(EMPHASIS MINE)

Saying these words: This is the blood that seals and ratifies the agreement (the testament, the covenant) which God commanded [me to deliver to] you.

—HEBREWS 9:20, AMP

Then he said, "This blood confirms the covenant God has made with you."

—HEBREWS 9:20, NLT

Testament and *covenant* are the same word in the Greek.[8] The blood was not only sprinkled on the vessels in the tabernacle, but also on the tabernacle. The tabernacle was the physical structure in which the Israelites worshipped God. You cannot afford to behave however you like in God's house, or to serve in the house of God while being actively in sin because the tabernacle of God is holy. God meets us on holy ground. We serve a holy God, and He has called us to holiness. Everything in the house of God is consecrated unto Him by the blood of Jesus!

In the New Testament, the believer is called the temple of God, so he cannot afford to be defiled, but must be holy as God is holy.

Know ye not that ye are the temple of God, and that the Spirit of God dwelleth in you? If any man defile the temple of God, him shall God destroy; for the temple of God is holy, which temple ye are.

—1 CORINTHIANS 3:16–17

> And what agreement hath the temple of God with
> idols? for ye are the temple of the living God; as God
> hath said, I will dwell in them, and walk in them;
> and I will be their God, and they shall be my people.
> —2 CORINTHIANS 6:16

That is why Jesus told the Samaritan woman in John
4:21 that worship of God is neither in the mountain nor at
Jerusalem. God is seeking true worshippers who worship
Him in spirit and in truth.

> And as they were eating, Jesus took bread, and
> blessed it, and brake it, and gave it to the disciples,
> and said, Take, eat; this is my body. And he took the
> cup, and gave thanks, and gave it to them, saying,
> Drink ye all of it; for this is my blood of the new
> testament, which is shed for many for the remission
> of sins.
> —MATTHEW 26:26–28

In Exodus 24:8, Moses talked about the blood of covenant, but in Matthew 26:28, Jesus calls it His blood of
the new covenant. The new covenant is ratified, confirmed,
and sealed by the blood of Jesus. When we say we are
reading the Old Testament or the New Testament, we are
actually saying that we are reading the Old Covenant or
New Covenant.

The Bible contains the covenants of God with man.
Therefore, whenever you are reading the Bible, you are not
just reading letters in black or red, but you are reading
God's Word which is covenant with you and sealed or confirmed by the blood of Jesus. No matter what is going on in
the world, nothing can change the Word of God. Instead,

it is the Word of God that has the ability to change all things. When you know that the Word of God is sealed by the blood of Jesus, then there is no place for doubt. There is no surer thing to confirm the Word of God than the sinless blood of Jesus Christ.

Covenant or *testament* in Greek is *diathéké* which means a disposition of property by will or otherwise—a promise or undertaking on the part of God.[9] God's Word is His promise, undertaking, or responsibility to you, and God does not lie or fail. God sees His Word as covenant with you, and He will not break His covenant or alter the thing that has gone forth from His lips. His Word is not outdated, but forever current because He is I AM. In contradiction to the English meaning of *covenant* which is a coming together—signifying a mutual undertaking between two parties or more, each binding himself to fulfill obligation—the Greek word *diathéké* does not in itself contain the idea of joint obligation. It mostly signifies an obligation undertaken by a single person. This means that in God's covenant with you, He is the One who does all things. Your role or responsibility is to believe His Word to you. You do not work for the promise of God or make it happen. As a child of God, you believe the promise of God because it is already confirmed and sealed by the blood of Jesus. You are to see God's Word to you as His promise to you, His covenant with you!

An example that readily comes to mind is in the Old Testament when God told the Israelites, through Moses, that He was going to smite all the first-born males of the Egyptians, but would spare them. The sparing of their lives was God's promise to the Israelites. He told them to put the blood of the lamb on the doorposts and lintels of their homes, and the death angel would pass over. The blood was a confirmation and seal of God's promise. He also told them not to go out that night but to stay in their homes within the confines of the blood. God spoke the promise to His people and sealed it by the blood. The Word of God goes hand in hand with the blood of Jesus. You cannot separate the two. Moses sprinkled the book of the law and the people with the blood. The blood is not only on you, but it is also on the Word of God. On the cross, the blood of Jesus was on Jesus, who is the Word of God. Each time you go to the Word, see the blood of Jesus. The Word of God must come to pass. God is in covenant relationship with us through the blood of Jesus. When a couple exchanges marriage vows at the altar, these vows are their promises to each other. They ratify or confirm their vows by their wedding rings. God has given us the sinless blood of Jesus, which defeated the devil, to ratify or confirm His Word to us. Why should you believe the Word of God? Because God's Word is already confirmed, and as the blood of Jesus is on the Word of God, the devil cannot touch it. On the communion table, you have the body and blood of Jesus Christ—the Word and the blood. Ask the Lord to give you a revelation of the blood of Jesus.

During one of our prayer meetings as we were singing about the blood of Jesus, the Lord started asking me these questions, "How much of the blood do you want? How much of the blood do you desire? That's a question only you can answer. How much of the blood do you desire? How much? How much? Because it is available to you. How much of the blood do you want? Do you just want a trickle? Do you want a pool? Do you want just a splash? Do you just want a sprinkling? How much of the blood do you want? Because it is available to you. Whatever amount you want is available to you. But the question is, 'How much of the blood do you want?'" Then I started praying that the Father would open the eyes of our understanding that we might perceive even these questions that He was asking us. He continued speaking to me: "How much? How much? How much? How far will you allow the blood go in your life? What is the demand you put on the blood, because if there is something that hell fears and is afraid of—it is the blood of Jesus. The blood of Jesus not only speaks of the victory of Jesus but it also speaks of the defeat of the enemy. The enemy cannot stand the blood of Jesus because everything about the blood is for you. So I am going to ask that question again. How much of the blood of Jesus do you want? How far will you allow the blood of Jesus go into your affairs? How much do you want the blood of Jesus to speak on your behalf? The blood of the One who won victory over death. The blood of the One who won victory over sin. How much of His blood do you desire?"

I then started praying that the Father would just give us the revelation and understanding of the blood which got our victory. An understanding of the blood that brought our redemption and our salvation. An understanding of the blood that the enemy has no antidote to. An understanding of the blood that speaks mercy continually on our behalf. An understanding of the blood that will go as far as we allow it to go. An understanding of the blood that speaks. An understanding of the blood in which is the life of Jesus Christ. An understanding of the sinless blood of Jesus Christ. Then the Lord spoke this to my spirit: "The blood is for My church. How far will you allow the blood of Jesus go into your ministry? How far? How far and how wide? How much will you allow the blood to speak on your behalf? Because the blood speaks for the saints of God as that was the ransom price. How much will you allow the blood to help you not to go back into your captivity? How much will you allow the blood to do a work on your behalf in your household? How much will you present the blood of Jesus before your enemies? Have you ever thought of that—of presenting the blood before your enemies?"

Then in my spirit, I saw that some people that entered the sanctuary that morning had come in with chains on them, but as we were singing about the blood, I saw those chains falling off because bondage cannot remain where the blood of Jesus is. That is why the Lord was asking us how much we will allow the blood to work on our behalf because where the blood is, there can be no captivity. Where the blood is, the enemy can never win. Where the blood is, the enemy can never prevail; there can be no activity of the enemy. Where the blood is, the enemy is disallowed.

Then, I heard the Spirit of the Lord say, "It seems as if the church of Christ has forgotten about the blood. If you had not forgotten about the blood, then you would speak about it all the time. It was given up for you." We are to speak about that which was given up for us, that wrought our salvation and redemption—the blood that continues to speak and has a place in the heavenly tabernacle. The Word of God says that Jesus entered the heavenly Holy of holies by His own blood. The blood will enter in on your behalf. The blood will bring you heavenly counsel. The council of heaven will sit on your behalf because of the blood. The blood defends even without your knowing it;

it is speaking on your behalf in the heavenly council and says, "There must be mercy for this one." Oh, the blood of Jesus!

The Lord is looking for a church that is delivered and free to fully understand all that Christ has done for it because therein is our victory. When you are not fully aware of what He has done for you, how can you lay claim to it? How can you walk in it? How can you see it? How can you come to an understanding of it? How can you perceive it? How can you pass on the knowledge to others when you don't fully understand? Understanding is found at the throne of God, and the blood gives you access to the throne of grace—the place where you find divine ability for all that God has called you to. Access cannot be denied you because of the blood. So how much are you going to allow the blood speak on your behalf?

Begin to raise the blood in your circumstances. Begin to raise the blood in your situations. Begin to raise the blood in your household. Begin to raise the blood in your workplace. Begin to raise the blood in your walk with the Lord. Begin to speak the blood into all things in your life. On Jesus' body on the cross of Calvary, there was no place the blood didn't cover. He was completely covered in His blood. That is the picture of the redeemed church of Christ: everything from head to toe is covered by the blood. The enemy cannot touch anything covered by the blood of Jesus.

Afterward, I saw in my spirit the chains coming off people; then I started hearing the Holy Spirit say, "Tell the people to claim their healing by the blood—the sinless blood of Jesus Christ." The Word of God says the life is in the blood. There is no infirmity in the life of Jesus and in His blood. There is no sickness; there is no bacteria in the blood of Jesus. There is no generational curse in the blood of Jesus. There is no generational disease in the blood of Jesus, so begin to claim your inheritance in the blood. Jesus has given us His blood; He has given us His life. See the blood of Jesus in your situation or infirmity and take hold of your healing. There is nothing on planet Earth that the blood of Jesus does not have an answer to. It speaks the mercy of God. It speaks the life of Christ that overcame all, even death and the tomb. Jesus lives forevermore; therefore, there is life forevermore in His blood.

Maybe you have a family history of illness—it was in your grandparents, in your parents, and you expect it to be in you. The blood stops it; the blood removes it; the blood erases it. Remind the enemy that you are no longer of that family line; you are now in the family line of God. All that mess in the family line cannot get into you and your seed. When an exchange blood transfusion is done for an individual, all his blood is removed, and he is transfused with the donor's blood. As a believer, you have had an exchange blood transfusion in the spirit—it is just for you to receive what the Lord Jesus has done for you.

If you have a rebellious child who does not have an ear to hear, start raising the blood of Jesus in the life of that child. Start exchanging everything in that child's life with the blood of Jesus and allow the blood to disengage him from every ungodly act.

Jesus Christ with His blood entered hell and took all the keys from the devil. You can take all the keys with the blood. Keys of destruction and keys of death are removed by the blood. Revelation 19:13 talks about Jesus Christ's vesture being dipped in His blood, the Lamb that was slain before the foundation of the world. The Greek word for *dip* is *baptó*, from which the word *baptizó*, which means to baptize, is derived.[10] Jesus is wearing vesture baptized in His own blood.

> But I have a baptism to be baptized with; and how
> am I straitened till it be accomplished!
>
> —LUKE 12:50

The blood speaks in every realm. It is only with the mind of Christ that you can understand what Christ has done for you. There is mental, physical, emotional, and financial healing in the blood of Jesus. I want you to see healing in the blood and say, "Healing is mine." There is victory in the blood of Jesus. It protects you from every evil work and brings you into your place and walk in destiny. It harnesses you in faith.

The Lord has given us this beautiful helmet of salvation. Are you wearing it? If you are not wearing it and a situation arises, you will not be able to agree with the Word of God. Instead, your word will be in agreement with the devil, and you will lose your head in the heat of battle. Put on the helmet of salvation! Declare that you have a sound mind. Declare that you shall not be lazy in reading the Word of God, but you shall become a student of the Word of God, diligently studying it to get the rhéma word and revelation knowledge of your salvation. This becomes a strong helmet upon your head so that the enemy can no longer penetrate your thoughts. Declare that your mind is sanctified by the Word of God, and that you are no longer passive, but active in rejecting the thoughts from the evil one. Declare that you shall not lose your head in battle, but you shall see situations through God's Word and walk in the wisdom of God. Declare that your mouth is a well of life, speaking life and not death into situations. Declare that you have become one with the Word of God. Jesus said that as He hears His Father speak, so He speaks. What you see and read in the Word is what you speak. It is the Word of God made flesh that God sent to save humankind, and the Word of God is still able to save. Declare that you have ears to hear the Word of God, and with each act of hearing, faith will continue to rise in your life.

ENDNOTES

1. *Perikephalaia*, "helmet," Strong's G4030.

2. *Peri* ("around"), *kephale* ("head"), Strong's G4012, G2776.

3. *Zoar*, "little, insignificant, small," Strong's H6820.

4. *Bela*, "destruction, swallower, devourer," Strong's H1105.

5. *El Shaddai*, Strong's H7706.

6. *Of*, "origin," Strong's G1537.

7. *Ekpíptō*, "fails," Strong's G1601.

8. *Diathéké*, "covenant, testament," Strong's G1242.

9. *Diathéké*, "covenant, testament," *Vine's Expository Dictionary*, 250.

10. *Baptó*, "dip," *Vine's Expository Dictionary*, 313.

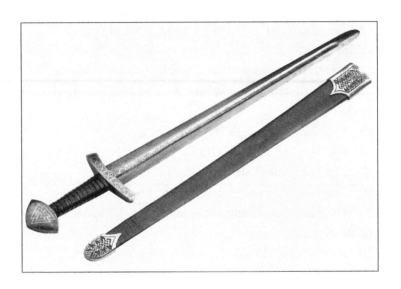

Chapter 7

SWORD *of the* SPIRIT

And take the helmet of salvation, and the
sword of the Spirit, which is the word of God.
—EPHESIANS 6:17

THE GREEK WORD for *word* in this verse is *rhéma*.[1] What is rhéma? Rhéma is the spoken or revealed Word of God by the Holy Spirit. The rhéma of God is the sword of the Spirit! It is not the sword of the flesh or of man, but of the Spirit. Sometimes, when we are going through situations, instead of using the sword of the Spirit, we use the sword of man or the sword of our flesh which is carnality by saying unseasoned words and exhibiting immature behavior to try to tackle the situation. The sword that God has given us as a part of the whole armor of God is the sword of the Spirit. Why? Ephesians 6:12 says that our warfare is not against flesh and blood but against principalities, against powers, against the rulers of the darkness of this world, against spiritual wickedness in high places. So the warfare is in the spirit and should be done through the Spirit of God.

Romans 10:8 says that the Word (rhéma) is nigh you, even in your mouth, and in your heart—that is, the Word of faith. This means that rhéma is not head knowledge. For you to speak the Word of faith, the Word has to first be in your heart. This means that it has to first move from head knowledge to heart knowledge. This requires not just a *deposit* of the Word in the heart, but an *abundance*, because from the abundance of the heart, the mouth speaks. The Word in your heart has to overflow into your speaking. That is why, if your heart is not abundant with the Word of God and overflowing with it, when you are in a crisis situation, the first thing you speak will not be the Word, but whatever your heart is full of. However, when your heart is filled and overflowing with the Word, in whichever situation you find yourself, whether it is a mountaintop or valley experience, the first thing that will issue forth from your mouth will be the Word of faith.

When you speak the Word of faith, you are speaking a decree or command because there is no doubt. That is why the Word of faith is rhéma and not logos. When you speak the Word of faith, you do not have to explain to anyone why you believe what you believe. All you know is that the Word must come to pass, because it has been processed from logos to rhéma. You do not speak the Word of faith because you have a degree in theology, but because the Holy Spirit has revealed the Word to you as it relates to your circumstance, and this revelation is burned and engraved in your heart. From this heart knowledge birthed out of intimacy with the Holy Spirit, you speak the Word. Therefore, when people ask you why you believe it will come to pass, you say, "Because I have spoken it." This is because what you have spoken is the Word of faith.

> That if thou shalt confess with thy mouth the Lord
> Jesus [*who is the Word of God*], and shalt believe
> in thine heart that God hath raised him from the
> dead, thou shalt be saved. For with the heart man
> believeth unto righteousness; and with the mouth
> confession is made unto salvation.
>
> —ROMANS 10:9–10
> (EMPHASIS MINE)

There has to be a synergistic action between your heart and mouth. The act of believing God's Word in your heart is viewed by God as righteousness. Therefore, when anything contrary to that Word is taking place in your life, the Lord fights on your behalf because you have brought yourself into a position of right standing with Him through believing His Word in your heart. Do you now see why the enemy does not want you to believe God's Word? By believing God's Word, you are already in the right position for victory. It is from this position of victory that you speak. When you speak a word that you do not believe, you are not on the ground of righteousness; therefore, you are not in a place where you will have victory. You speak from the position of righteousness through your heart belief of the word, and so what you speak is the Word of faith that must deliver and save.

When you speak faith-filled words, you are speaking life and therefore light. When you speak words contrary to the Word of God, you are speaking death and therefore darkness. Death and life are in the power of the tongue (Prov. 18:21). The entrance (opening, disclosure) of God's Word into your situation brings light and gives understanding to the simple (Ps. 119:130). In Genesis 1:2, God saw that the Earth was without form and void and darkness was upon it. He did not desire this, so He spoke light forth. Are you speaking what you see, or are you speaking life and therefore light?

Do not change your confession of the surety of God's deliverance for you because you have a faithful and great High Priest, Jesus Christ, who has passed on to the heavens. He is at God's right hand in the seat of power and authority, forever interceding on your behalf. Be in total submission to the will of God, knowing that in Him, you have an expected future, hope, and end (Jer. 29:11). Your soul needs to be stilled and quieted like that of a weaned child (Ps. 131:2). A weaned child does not fret or panic when he does not see his mother around. In your time of pain, when your flesh does not feel God's presence, you need to behave as a weaned child, cleaving onto and confessing God's Word, knowing that He will never leave you or forsake you. The Lord teaches weaned believers knowledge in the way they should go and causes them to understand doctrine or kingdom principles (Isa. 28:9). There are too many unweaned saints in the body of Christ.

The word *confess* in Greek is *homologeó,* which is a combination of two words: *homou* which means "same," and *logos* which means "word."[2] Therefore, to "*homologeó* with your mouth" means to say exactly the same word God has said about the situation with your mouth and nothing else. You continue saying it till the situation conforms to the Word of God. In this manner, you are in correct alignment with the Godhead. In the tabernacle, one had to go from the outer court to the inner court or Holy place and then into the Holy of holies. In the Holy place, there was the table of shewbread and the seven lampsticks—and in the middle was the altar of incense. You had to pass by the altar of incense to go into the Holy of holies to enter God's presence. You could not go from either side of the Holy place to enter the Holy of holies. You had to stand in the middle, in direct alignment with the altar of incense, to do this. With the finished work of Christ on the cross, the veil has been torn. The veil was not torn from the bottom up, but from the top to the bottom, so it had to be done by a hand from heaven—and what God has torn, no one can put together again. The way to the Holy of holies is eternally open to the child of God who believes. When we read the Word of God, believe it in our heart, and speak what we believe, which is the Word of faith, we immediately bring ourselves in the spirit to right standing in the place of the altar of incense. We can then enter into the Holy of holies through our worship of God. Believing God is an act of worship. When we believe God, we honor Him. Romans 10:9–10 says that your spoken word is an overflow of what you have believed in your heart and causes you to walk in God's righteousness, salvation, and deliverance! The Bible describes those who do not believe God's Word as wicked and evil before God because when you doubt God's Word, you are telling Him that He is a liar, and this is sin.

Therefore, continually speak rhéma—the believed Word of God as revealed by the Holy Spirit. Jesus, the Word of God, God the Father, and the Holy Spirit move together, and they are always in oneness. In Genesis 1:2, we are told that the world was completely covered with water and in utter chaos and darkness. The Holy Spirit hovered over the face of the Earth and could not act till God spoke the Word! When you speak the believed Word of God as revealed by the Holy Spirit, you enter into the realm of creativity and miracles. We are told in Hebrews 4:12 that the

Word of God is quick, and powerful, and sharper than any two-edged sword, piercing even to the dividing asunder of soul and spirit, and of the joints and marrow, and is a discerner of the thoughts and intents of the heart. Goliath had a gigantic sword, but David spoke the Word of the Lord which is sharper than any two-edged sword. David had a purpose for wanting to kill Goliath. This was so that all the Earth would know that there is a God in Israel who saves not with sword or spear, for the battle is the Lord's (1 Sam. 17:46–47). Purpose forges stability in the time of battle. Knowing the purpose of a need always produces prayer, which leads to perception (knowing when, where, and how), which produces power.

The Greek word for *word* in Hebrews 4:12 is *logos*.[3] You have to have logos, the written Word of God before it becomes rhéma, the revealed Word of God by the Holy Spirit. The Greek word for *sword* in Hebrews 4:12 is *machaira*, the same word used for sword in Ephesians 6:17.[4] The machaira pierces to cause separation between the soul and spirit, the joints and marrow, and is a discerner of the thoughts and intents of the heart. This means that there is nothing that the Word of God cannot pierce and separate. That is why we need to be people of the Word of God. The word *machaira* is derived from the word maché meaning a battle or controversy."[5] Holding the machaira meant you were ready for a fight. It is light and can be used with one hand; it is maneuvered quickly with ease, thereby allowing the other hand to be free to hold the shield. It was used in close hand-to-hand combat. Its action is cutting and thrusting. It is a short sword with a strong, slightly backward, curved blade whose shape is like a lion's claw. The lion of Judah resides in you!

All lions have retractable claws. This helps them keep their claws razor sharp. If they could not retract their claws, continuous contact with the ground would cause the claws to lose their sharpness and become blunt. When lions are just going on a stroll or walking up and down, they keep their claws retracted. In this way, they retain the sharpness of their claws. We should be people who are continually in the spirit. You might say to yourself, "But I go to work." You can still be in the spirit. This is practicing the presence of God. God is always God and does not go on holiday from being God. We need to ensure that we are continually sharpened in our spirits through the quickening power of the Word of God. When everything is going well for us, we have a tendency to read the Bible less and reduce our prayers, since there is no trouble. On the contrary, that is when we should read and have more of the Word of God because that is when we are more vulnerable. Do you think the devil is happy when all is going well with you? We need to be people who are wise. The lion only brings out its claws when it is fighting. Lions often hunt very large animals, which are difficult to control because of their weight; they must hold onto them tightly so that the animal will not slip away. The sharper the claws, the stronger and steadier will be the lion's grip so that it can devour the animal. We should not run away from the devil, but deal with situations as they come our way with the Word of faith—and we must have a firm grip on the devil's neck. How do we do this? By speaking and living the Word.

In Joshua 5:13, the Lord appeared to Joshua as Captain of the Lord's host with His sword drawn in His hand and not in its sheath. When a soldier's sword is drawn, it means he is not ceremonially dressed, but battle ready. The whole armor of God is not a ceremonial dressing, but a dressing for combat. When a soldier goes to battle, his sword needs to be in his hand. Children of God are to do likewise. The rhéma of God needs to be in your hand, and you need to be battle ready with it.

> Through faith we understand that the worlds were framed by the word of God, so that things which are seen were not made of things which do appear.
>
> —HEBREWS 11:3

The Greek word for *framed* is *katartizó* which means to complete thoroughly, repair, restore, prepare, or set in order.[6] The Word of God in this verse is *rhéma*. The scripture does not say "things which are seen were made from the unseen," but "things which are seen were not made of things which do appear or which we presently see." Some of us are so focused on what we see that we get depressed and discouraged when they do not line up with our desire. If we know that what we want or need to see is completely dependent on rhéma, then we will not magnify the contrary things we see by meditating on them. Instead, we will spend time meditating on logos so that we can convert it to rhéma, because it is rhéma that delivers, saves, and is the sword of the Spirit. It is rhéma that defeats the devil. We restore and complete thoroughly what we desire by rhéma.

How do we move from logos to rhéma? How do we move from the written Word; the Word we read on the pages of the Bible, to rhéma; the spoken Word revealed by the Holy Spirit? In Joshua 1:8, God gave Joshua important instructions for his success as a leader of the people. Joshua was told to meditate on the Word of God day and night. Some of us meditate on the Word of God only at weekends since we are so busy during the week. What a shame! Some do so twice a week, but the Bible tells us to do so every day— and not just once a day, but day and night. To meditate does not mean for you to blank out your mind. To meditate means to ponder, mutter, utter, and roar. First read the written Word of God and use a Bible concordance and dictionary. Thank God, the internet has many good tools you can use to research the Bible. You will want to know the original meaning of the words. In the Old Testament, the words were in Hebrew, and in the New Testament, Greek. You will also want to know under what circumstances the Word was spoken and what civilization was like then. Go into depth in the Word of God. We go into depth about our mode of dressing, cooking, the country we want to visit on our next holiday, etc. Why can we not go into depth about the Word of God that is our life? You can do all this research while asking the Holy Spirit to direct you and reveal the Word of God to you because the greatest and best revealer of the Word of God is the Holy Spirit. The Holy Spirit teaches you the Word.

It is what the Holy Spirit hears from Jesus that He tells you, and Jesus is the Word of God (John 16:13–14). When you want to understand a book, you often want to meet the author to ask him what was in his mind when he wrote the book. The Holy Spirit tells you what the Word, Jesus, says about the Word. You have to cooperate with the Holy Spirit. You cannot be reading the Word and shut off the Holy Spirit; otherwise, you will end up confused and have no understanding of the Word. The Word of God is spirit and life, and it is only the Spirit of God that can explain it to you. It does not matter whether you have PhD in theology. As you cooperate with the Holy Spirit, any time you read the Word of God, invite the Holy Spirit to teach and instruct you and open your mind to revelation of the Word. The Word of God is sperm (seed), and each time you encounter it by your spirit through the Holy Spirit, it impregnates your spirit with its revelation. You should always be pregnant in your spirit with the revelation of the Word of God. Your spirit through the Holy Spirit connects you to the life in the Word of God, which is the life of God. This does not take place in one minute, but it takes time. As you do this, start pondering in your heart whatever the Holy Spirit drops in your spirit about the Word you are reading. When the angel Gabriel told Mary about the birth of Jesus and what God was going to use her to do, she pondered on these things. When the shepherds came, she pondered on what they spoke. Like Mary, you also should ponder on what the Holy Spirit speaks to you.

Do you know that the Word of God is precious? You need to treat it as precious and be attentive to what the Holy Spirit speaks to you. Write down what He speaks to you because you do not want to add to it or remove from it. Every believer needs to have a prayer journal. If you are speaking to the Holy Spirit and you do not have writing materials with you, then you have not prepared yourself to receive. There is no greater treasure than the Word of God. Wherever you are, cooking in the kitchen, getting ready for work, in the bathroom, driving your car, or in between your daily schedule, ponder on the Word of God. Keep going over and over in your mind the revelation of the Word that the Holy Spirit has dropped in your spirit. As you begin to ponder, the Holy Spirit will flood the eyes of your understanding with light pertaining to the

Word, and as you begin to receive this, you will begin to mutter. Mutter the revealed Word under your breath (the Jews mutter the Word of God at the Wailing Wall); as you mutter, your ears are open to the Word of God because hearing comes by the Word of God.

What you hear in the world plugs your ears to God, but what you hear through the Word opens your ears to God. As you continue to mutter, faith comes by hearing the spoken Word of God that resulted from your meditation on the Word. You are not to wait for the pastor to preach before you hear the Word. Belief for the Word rises in your heart, and as this happens, you are no longer muttering, but uttering. You are no longer whispering under your breath, but you are uttering because you are convinced of what you are speaking. You believe, so you speak. As you begin to utter (say, speak), a quickening comes in your spirit because the Word of God enlivens. The Word goes through every fiber of your being, and then you begin to roar in your spirit by speaking in the language that the Holy Spirit has given you—tongues. You begin to see the hedge coming up around your house, your child coming out of the contrary set-up, your boss having a change of heart, or whatever you believe God for because you have muttered, uttered, and now you are roaring in the spirit. What you speak forth is rhéma and must come to pass because it is the revealed Word you have believed in your heart—and because you believe, so you speak (2 Cor. 4:13).

> For as the rain cometh down, and the snow from heaven, and returneth not thither, but watereth the earth, and maketh it bring forth and bud, that it may give seed to the sower, and bread to the eater: So shall my word be that goeth forth out of my

mouth: it shall not return unto me void, but it shall
accomplish that which I please, and it shall prosper
in the thing whereto I sent it.
—ISAIAH 55:10–11

Let us look at the analogy being made in this scripture.
Rain and snow come from heaven, and when they do so,
they do not go back. Have you ever seen raindrops come
halfway down, suddenly change their minds, and say to
themselves, "We think we better go back up to heaven"?
Once they come down, they come right down to the earth.
The same thing happens with snow. Likewise, the Word
of God going forth out of God's mouth does not return
to God empty, just as the rain and snow come down for
a purpose; which is to water the earth to remove dryness
and barrenness. As a result, the rain and snow make the
earth bring forth fruit to give seed to the sower and bread
to the eater. This means that the earth brings forth life
with purpose that blesses others. Therein, the purpose of
the rain and snow watering the earth is fulfilled. The deci-
sion whether or not to bring forth fruit is no longer the
earth's, but that of the rain and snow which make it do so.
That is why you need to speak rhéma, because it operates
under a higher law as you also belong to a higher kingdom,
the kingdom of God. The spoken Word of God does not
return to God empty, but accomplishes that which God
pleases and prospers in the thing that God sent it. What
pleases God? He pleases in His Word being done. The
word *accomplish* does not mean to start and stop halfway,
but to complete from start to finish. That is why Jesus said
to those who were coming against Him that He had come
to do the work His Father sent Him and to accomplish
it (John 4:34). Jesus said on the cross, "It is finished." We

need to confess the Word of God all the time. It will also prosper and not be a hidden thing when it comes to pass.

Let us see some more things that rhéma does.

Saves / Delivers

Second Timothy 3:16 says that all scripture is given by inspiration of God. This means that all scripture is inspirited by God, i.e., all scripture has the breath of God in it because the Spirit of God is the breath of God. God breathed His Spirit into man, and man became a living soul. Therefore, when you speak rhéma, you are directing the breath of God to that thing or person or situation to which you speak it. God's power is expressed by His word. The Greek word for *deliver* is *exaireo* which means "pluck out" or "rescue."[7] The breath of God is directed in the spoken word (rhéma), which is His power to lift you out of that situation or blow that situation off from you. Rhéma plucks you out and rescues your destiny because it has the breath of God in it. The gospel of Christ is the power of God unto salvation unto all who believe with their heart to righteousness and speak the rhéma of God (Rom. 1:16).

Upholds / Carries You

> Who being the brightness of his glory, and the express image of his person, and upholding all things by the word of his power, when he had by himself purged our sins, sat down on the right hand of the Majesty on high.
> —HEBREWS 1:3

Jesus upholds, carries, or bears all things by the word (rhéma) of His power. In Romans 1:16, we are told that the gospel of Christ is the power of God unto salvation. An example of the Word of God carrying one is seen in Matthew 14:26–29 when the disciples were in a boat and there was a storm. The weather was contrary to them. Jesus had been praying on the mountain, and then at the fourth watch of the night, He came to them walking on water. When the disciples saw Jesus walking on water, they were scared, being filled with fright. The disciples thought, "Is this a ghost? What is happening here? We are in a bad enough situation, but what form are we seeing coming toward us?" Peter now said, "Lord, if that is you, bid me to come." Jesus' word to Peter was, "Come." Peter believed this word in his heart, and he acted on it. The word (rhéma) of Jesus' power carried Peter and enabled him to walk on water, and by so doing, he walked on the impossible. It does not matter how difficult or bad the situation you are in is; rhéma will carry you. When Peter was walking on the water, he was looking at Jesus, the author and finisher of his faith. When you are walking on rhéma, there is only one place you can focus your heart and mind on: Jesus, because He is the author and finisher of your faith. It was when Peter's gaze shifted from Jesus, because of the noise of the enemy manifested by the tumultuous weather conditions, that he doubted the word "come" and started to sink.

Sustains Life

> But he answered and said, It is written, Man shall not live by bread alone, but by every word that pro-
> ceedeth out of the mouth of God.
>
> —MATTHEW 4:4

We live by rhéma. There are some people who know the Word from Genesis to Revelation, but it is all logos and not rhéma. For such, it is impossible to live the God-kind of life. We live the abundant life of Christ by every rhéma that proceeds out of the mouth of God. How do you get your job? By rhéma. How do you stay in the workplace when there are so many devils around you? By rhéma. How do you prosper? By rhéma. How did Jesus defeat the devil when he came to tempt Him? By rhéma.

Causes or Brings Provision

> Now when he had left speaking, he said unto Simon, Launch out into the deep, and let down your nets for a draught. And Simon answering said unto him, Master, we have toiled all the night, and have taken nothing: nevertheless at thy word I will let down the net. And when they had this done, they inclosed a great multitude of fishes: and their net brake.
>
> —Luke 5:4–6

Rhéma will bring provision to your life. Therefore, instead of lamenting about your lack, start speaking *rhéma* and let it bring a change for good in your situation.

Gives Light and Understanding

> The entrance of thy words giveth light; it giveth understanding unto the simple.
>
> —Psalm 119:130

The word *entrance* in Hebrew is *pethach* which means opening or disclosure.[8] The opening or disclosure of God's Word gives light and understanding to the simple. Rhéma gives light and understanding in situations. In Genesis 1:31, we are told that God did not start creating anything in darkness till He spoke light into existence because the light of God is the life of men. In His light is life. It is the light of God that sustains life. That is why you cannot afford any darkness in your life—because wherever there is darkness, there is death. Your life needs to be flooded with the light of God. What happens to a plant that is kept in a dark place? No matter how beautiful it is initially, it will die when kept in a dark place because it needs light for photosynthesis. The only life that can exist where the light of God is present is the life of God.

Joshua was told by God that the Word of God was not to depart from his mouth. Do not stop speaking the Word of God. There must always be rhéma in your mouth, and this only comes from meditating on the Word of God day and night. Meditation on the Word of God leads to the Word of God being mixed with faith which causes us to profit. What we speak is rhéma and must bring forth (Heb. 4:2). It will never return to God void.

Start thanking the Lord for His Word; without the logos, there would be no rhéma. Thank Him for the treasure and the enablement He has given you through His Word. When God decided to redeem humankind, there was no one better God could send than the Word of God. Bring yourself in submission to the Word of God this day and every day of your life. Stand firm in truth, righteousness, peace, salvation, faith, and the Word of God. The whole armor of God is Jesus. Put on Jesus (Rom. 13:12, 14).

That this book is coming into your hands now is not a coincidence; it is by the divine providence of God. If you do not have a relationship with the Lord Jesus Christ and you want one, please say the prayer below.

Dear Jesus, I come to You today acknowledging that I am a sinner. I confess my sins this day and receive You as my Lord and Savior. I believe that You are the Son of God. I believe that You went to the cross on my behalf and died for my sins. I believe that You were buried and on the third day arose from the dead. I believe that You are now seated at the right hand of God the Father in heaven, forever interceding on my behalf. Today I am born again and grafted into the family of God through Your blood.

If you have previously given your life to Jesus Christ but strayed away and the life you now live is at variance with the Word of God, please say the prayer below.

Lord Jesus, I confess my sins of rebellion toward You and God the Father. Please forgive me and cleanse me of all unrighteousness. I repent of every evil work I have done and for not having allowed my life to give You glory. I come to You today to rededicate my life and ask You to reconcile me back to God my Father. Thank You.

ENDNOTES

1. *Rhéma*, "word," Strong's G4487.
2. *Homologeó*, "confess," Strong's G3670.
3. *Logos*, "word," Strong's G3056.
4. *Machaira*, "sword," Strong's G3162.
5. *Maché*, "battle, controversy," Strong's 3163.
6. *Katartizó*, "framed," Strong's G2675.
7. *Exaireo*, "deliver," *Vine's Expository Dictionary*, 289.
8. *Pethach*, "entrance," Strong's H6608.

ABOUT *the* AUTHOR

D R. EKI AGHAHOWA was ordained to the work of Gospel ministry on February 9, 2006, and is the Senior Pastor of Seed of Life World Ministries, Kuwait. She is a radiologist by profession and has a Ministerial Diploma from Vision International University, Ramona, California. She counts her relationship with the Lord as the most important thing in her life and has a passion to nurture believers to be disciples of Jesus doing the works of Christ. She is also the author of *It Is Finished*, *Understanding the Holy Spirit*, and *Seeking God's Kingdom*. Dr. Aghahowa is listed in the Marquis Who's Who in the World. She has three daughters and a grandson.

CONTACT *the* AUTHOR

For further information, please contact the author at:

Seed of Life World Ministries
P.O. Box 2320
Duluth, GA 30096-9998

Email: eki_aghahowa2008@yahoo.com
Website: www.solwmkuwait.org

Made in the USA
Monee, IL
17 February 2024

53679044R00134